Abiding in Christ

Andrew Murray

Books by Andrew Murray

From Bethany House Publishers
With Updated Language

Abiding in Christ

Andrew Murray

BETHANYHOUSE

a division of Baker Publishing Group
Minneapolis, Minnesota

© 2003 by Bethany House Publishers

Published by Bethany House Publishers
11400 Hampshire Avenue South
Bloomington, Minnesota 55438
www.bethanyhouse.com

Bethany House Publishers is a division of
Baker Publishing Group, Grand Rapids, Michigan

Newly edited and updated for today's reader by Jeanne Hedrick.
Originally published in 1895 by Henry Altemus under the title *Abide in Christ.*

Printed in the United States of America

ISBN 978-0-7642-2762-2

Library of Congress Cataloging-in-Publication Data
Murray, Andrew, 1828–1917.
   [Abide in Christ]
   Abide in Christ / by Andrew Murray.
      p. cm.
   Originally published: Abide in Christ. Philadelphia, Pa. : H. Altemus, 1895.
   ISBN 0-7642-2762-9 (pbk.)
   1. Meditations. 2. Christian life—Reformed authors. I. Title.
BV4832.3.M87   2003
248.4—dc21   2002155876

Cover design by Eric Walljasper

In keeping with biblical principles of creation stewardship, Baker Publishing Group advocates the responsible use of our natural resources. As a member of the Green Press Initiative, our company uses recycled paper when possible. The text paper of this book is composed in part of post-consumer waste.

19   20   21   22   23   24   25   21   20   19   18   17   16   15

ANDREW MURRAY was born in South Africa in 1828. After receiving his education in Scotland and Holland, he returned to Africa and spent many years as a missionary pastor. He and his wife, Emma, raised eight children. He is best known for his many devotional books, including some of the most enduring classics of Christian literature.

Preface

During Jesus' life on earth, the phrase He used most often when speaking of the relationship of the disciples to himself was "Follow Me." When about to leave for heaven, He gave them a new phrase, which better described their more intimate and spiritual union with himself in glory: "Abide in Me."

Unfortunately there are many earnest followers of Jesus who fail to grasp the full meaning of these words. While trusting Him for pardon and help, and seeking to some extent to obey Him, they have not realized the closeness of union, the intimacy of fellowship, or the wondrous oneness of life and interest He invites them to when He says, "Abide in Me." This is not only an unspeakable loss to them personally but also a great loss to the church and the world around them.

If we ask why those who have accepted the Savior, and have experienced the renewing of the Holy Spirit, come short of the full salvation prepared for them, I am sure the answer will in many cases be ignorance, which leads to unbelief. If the reality of abiding in Christ, the living union with Him, the experience of His daily and hourly presence and keeping, were preached in our orthodox churches with the same distinctness and urgency as is His Atonement and our pardon through His blood, no doubt many would accept with gladness the invitation to such a life. And its influence would shine forth in the believers as they experience the purity and power, the love and joy, the fruit-bearing, and all the other blessings associated with abiding in Christ.

My desire to help those who have not yet fully understood what it means to abide in Him, or who have feared that it is a life beyond their reach, is why these meditations are now published. It is only by frequent repetition that a child learns its lessons. Only by continuously fixing the mind for a time on one of the lessons of faith is the believer gradually helped to take and thoroughly assimilate its benefits. I hope that to some, especially young believers, it will be a help to consider carefully the precious words, "Abide in Me," with the lessons connected with them in the parable of the Vine. Step by step we will see how truly this promise–precept is meant for us, how surely grace is provided to enable us to obey it, how indispensable the experience of its blessing is to a healthy Christian life, and how awesome are the blessings that flow from it. As we listen, meditate, and pray, the Holy Spirit will make the words to be spirit and life to us. This word of Jesus will become to us the power of God unto salvation, and through it will come the faith that grasps the long-desired blessing.

I pray earnestly that our gracious Lord may be pleased to bless this book, to help those who seek to know Him fully, as He has already blessed it in its original issue in the Dutch language. I pray that He would, by whatever means, make the multitudes of His dear children who are still living divided lives, to see how He claims them wholly for himself, and how wholehearted surrender to abide in Him alone brings a joy that is "unspeakable and full of glory" (1 Peter 1:8). May all of us who have begun to taste the sweetness of this life yield ourselves to be witnesses of the grace and power of our Lord to keep us united with Him. And may we seek by word and walk to win others to follow Him fully. It is only in such fruit-bearing that our own abiding can be maintained.

In conclusion, I would give one word of advice to my readers: It *takes time* to grow into Jesus the Vine; do not expect to abide in Him unless you will give Him that time. It is not enough to read God's Word, or meditations as found in this book; and when we think we understand the concepts and have asked God for His blessing, to go out in the hope that the blessing will remain. No, abiding requires day-by-day time with Jesus and the Father. We all know that we must take time for our meals each day. Every workman sets aside his time for dinner because it is important in his daily routine. In the same way, if we are to live through Jesus, we must feed on Him (John 6:57); we must thoroughly take in and assimilate the heavenly food the Father has given us in His life. Therefore, anyone who wants to learn to abide in Jesus must take time each day, before reading, while reading, and after reading, to put himself into contact with the living Jesus. He must yield himself distinctly and consciously to His blessed influence—giving Him the opportunity to take hold of him so that He may draw him up and keep him safe in His almighty life.

And now, to all God's children whom He allows me the privilege of pointing to the Heavenly Vine, I offer my fraternal love and greetings, with the prayer that to each one of them may be given the rich and full experience of abiding in Christ. And may the grace of Jesus, the love of God, and the fellowship of the Holy Spirit be their daily portion. Amen.

Contents

John 15:1-12

I am the true vine, and My Father is the vinedresser. Every branch in Me that does not bear fruit He takes away; and every branch that bears fruit He prunes, that it may bear more fruit. You are already clean because of the word which I have spoken to you. Abide in Me, and I in you. As the branch cannot bear fruit of itself, unless it abides in the vine, neither can you, unless you abide in Me. I am the vine, you are the branches. He who abides in Me, and I in him, bears much fruit; for without Me you can do nothing. If anyone does not abide in Me, he is cast out as a branch and is withered; and they gather them and throw them into the fire, and they are burned. If you abide in Me, and My words abide in you, you shall ask what you desire, and it shall be done for you. By this My Father is glorified, that you bear much fruit; so you will be My disciples. As the Father loved Me, I also have loved you; continue in My love. If you keep My commandments, you will abide in My love, just as I have kept My Father's commandments and abide in His love. These things I have spoken to you that My joy may remain in you, and that your joy may be full. This is My commandment, that you love one another as I have loved you.

All You Who Have Come to Him

Come to Me.

Matthew 11:28

Abide in Me.

John 15:4

It is to you who have heard and responded to the call, *"Come to Me,"* that this new invitation comes, *"Abide in Me."* The message comes from the same loving Savior. No doubt you have never regretted responding to His call and coming to Him. You experienced that His word was truth; all His promises He fulfilled; He made you a partaker of the blessings and the joy of His love. His welcome was heartfelt, His pardon full and free, His love most sweet and precious, was it not? You more than once, at your first coming to Him, had reason to say, "The half was not told me."

And yet you have had some disappointment. As time went on, your expectations were not always realized. The blessings you once enjoyed were lost; the love and joy of your first meeting with your Savior, instead of deepening, have become faint and weak. And you have often wondered why, with such a mighty and loving Savior, your experience of salvation was not a fuller one.

The answer is very simple. You wandered from Him. The blessings He bestows are all connected with His "Come to Me," and are only to be enjoyed in close fellowship with Him. You either did not fully understand, or did not rightly remember, that the call meant "Come to Me and remain with Me." This was His object and purpose when He first called you to himself. It was not to refresh you for a few short hours after your conversion with the joy of His love and deliverance, and then to send you forth to wander in sadness and sin. He destined you to something better than a short-lived blessing, to be enjoyed only in times of special earnestness and prayer, and then to pass away as you had to return to the more mundane duties of life.

No, indeed, He has prepared for you an abiding dwelling with himself, where your whole life and every moment of it might be spent and where the work of your daily life might be done as you enjoy unbroken communion with Him. This is what He meant when to that first word, "*Come* to Me," He added "*Abide* in Me." Just as earnest and faithful, as loving and tender, as the compassion contained in the invitation to "Come" was the grace that added a further invitation to "Abide." As mighty as the attraction with which that first word drew you were the bonds with which this second—had you but listened to it—would have kept you. And as great as were the blessings associated with coming, so much greater were the treasures to which abiding would have given you access.

Notice that He did not say, "Come to me and abide with

Me," but, "Abide *in* Me." The relationship was not only to be unbroken, but also intimate and complete. He opened His arms, to press you to himself; He opened His heart, to welcome you there; He opened up all His divine fullness of life and love, and offered to take you up into its fellowship, to make you wholly one with Him. There was a depth of meaning you have not yet realized in His words "Abide in Me."

Just as earnestly as He cried, "Come to Me," did He plead—had you but noticed it—"Abide in Me." Was it the fear of sin and its curse that first drew you to Him? The pardon you received on first coming could, with all the blessings flowing from it, only be confirmed and fully enjoyed by abiding in Him. Was it the longing to know and enjoy Infinite Love that was calling you? The first coming gave but single drops to taste; it is only the abiding that can really satisfy the thirsty soul and enable you to drink of the rivers of pleasure that are at His right hand (Psalm 16:11; 36:8). Was it the weary longing to be set free from the bondage of sin, to become pure and holy, and so find rest, the rest of God for the soul that drew you to Him? This too can only be realized as you abide in Him; only abiding in Jesus gives rest in Him. Or if it was the hope of an inheritance in glory, and an everlasting home in the presence of the Infinite One, the true preparation for this, as well as a taste of its glory in this life, is granted only to those who abide in Him.

The truth is, there is nothing that moved you to come that does not plead with even greater force: *Abide in Him.* You did well to come; you do better to abide. Who would be content, after seeking the King's palace, to stand in the door, when he is invited in to dwell in the King's presence, and share with Him in all the glory of His royal life? Let us enter in and abide, and enjoy fully all the rich supply His wondrous love has prepared for us!

I fear that there are many who have indeed come to Jesus, and who yet mournfully confess that they know little of this blessed abiding in Him. With some the reason is that they never fully understood that this was the meaning of the Savior's call. With others, though they heard the word, they did not know that such a life of abiding fellowship was possible and within their reach. Others will say that, though they did believe that such a life was possible, and seek after it, they have not yet discovered the secret of its attainment. And others, alas, will confess that it is their own unfaithfulness that has kept them from the enjoyment of the blessing. When the Savior would have kept them, they were not found ready to stay; they were not prepared to give up everything and to always, only, completely identify with Jesus.

To all such I come now in the name of Jesus, their Redeemer and mine, with the blessed message: "Abide in Me." In His name I invite them to come, and for a season meditate with me daily on its meaning, its lessons, its claims, and its promises. I know how many, and, to the young believer, how difficult, the questions are which suggest themselves in connection with the idea of abiding. There is especially the question to the possibility, in the midst of tiring work and continual distraction, of keeping up, or rather being kept in, abiding communion. I do not attempt to remove all difficulties; this Jesus Christ himself must do by His Holy Spirit.

What I will do, by the grace of God, is to repeat day by day the Master's blessed command, "Abide in Me," until it enters our hearts and finds a place there. In the light of Holy Scripture we should meditate on its meaning until the understanding, that gate to the heart, opens to grasp something of what it offers and expects. In this way we will discover the means of its attainment and learn what keeps us from it and what can help us to it. So we will feel its claims and be compelled to acknowledge that there can be no true allegiance to our King without simply and heartily accepting this important command.

Come, fellow believers, and let us day by day place ourselves at His feet, and meditate on this word of His with an eye fixed on Him alone. Let us set ourselves in quiet trust before Him, waiting to hear His holy voice—the still, small voice that is mightier than the storm that breaks the rocks—breathing its life-giving spirit within us as He speaks: "Abide in Me." The soul that hears *Jesus himself speak the word* receives with the word the power to accept and to hold the blessing He offers.

And may it please you, blessed Savior, to speak to us; let each of us truly hear your blessed voice. May the feeling of our deep need, and the faith of your wondrous love, combined with the sight of the wonderfully blessed life you are waiting to bestow upon us, compel us to listen and to obey as often as you speak: "Abide in Me." Let the answer from our heart day by day be ever clearer and fuller: "Blessed Savior, I do abide in you."

You Will Find Rest for Your Souls

Come to Me, all you who labor and are heavy laden, and I will
give you rest. Take My yoke upon you and learn from Me, for I
am gentle and lowly in heart, and you
will find rest for your souls.

Matthew 11:28–29

Rest for the soul: Such was the first promise extended by the
Savior to win the burdened sinner. Simple though it appears,
the promise is as large and comprehensive as can be found. Rest
for the soul—does it not imply deliverance from every fear, the
supply of every want, the fulfillment of every desire? And now
this is the prize with which the Savior woos back the wandering
one, the one who is mourning that his rest has not been so
abiding or so full as he had hoped, to return and abide in Him.
This was the reason that rest either has not been found, or, if
found, has been disturbed or lost again: you did not abide in
Him.

Have you ever noticed how, in the original invitation of the

Savior to come to Him (Matthew 11:28–29), the promise of rest was repeated twice, with such a variation in the conditions as might suggest that abiding rest can only be found in abiding nearness. First the Savior says, "Come to Me, and I will give you rest"; the very moment you come, and believe, I will give you rest, the rest of pardon and acceptance found in my love. But we know that all that God bestows needs time to become fully our own. It must be embraced, appropriated, and assimilated into our soul; without this not even Christ's giving can make it our own in terms of full experience and enjoyment.

And so the Savior repeats His promise, in words that clearly speak not so much of the initial rest with which He welcomes the weary one who comes, but of the deeper and personally appropriated rest of the soul that abides in Him. Now He not only says "Come to Me" but also "Take My yoke upon you and learn from Me"; become My scholars, yield yourselves to My training, submit in all things to My will, let your whole life be one with mine—in other words, abide in Me. And then He adds not only "I will give" but also "you will find rest for your souls." The *rest* that He gave at your first coming will become something you have really found and made your very own—the deeper, abiding rest which comes from longer acquaintance, closer fellowship, and entire surrender. "Take My yoke, and learn from Me," "Abide in Me"—this is the path to abiding rest.

These words of the Savior uncover what you have perhaps often wondered: How is it that the rest you at times enjoy is so often lost? This must have been the reason: You did not understand how *entire surrender to Jesus is the secret of perfect rest.* Giving up one's whole life to Him to rule and order, taking up His yoke, and allowing ourselves to be led and taught of Him, abiding in Him, to be and do only what He wills—these are the conditions of discipleship without which there can be no thought of maintaining the rest that was bestowed on first coming to Christ. This rest is in Christ, not something He gives apart from himself, and so it is only in having Him that the rest can really be kept and enjoyed.

It is because so many young believers fail to grasp this truth that their rest so quickly evaporates. With some it is that they really did not know; they were never taught how Jesus claims undivided allegiance of the whole heart and life. They were unaware that there is not a spot in the whole of life over which He does not wish to reign. They did not know how entire the consecration was that Jesus claimed. With others, who had some idea of what a very holy life a Christian ought to lead, the mistake was a different one: They could not believe such a life could be attained. Taking, bearing, and never for a moment laying aside the yoke of Jesus appeared to them to require such a strain of effort, and such an enormous amount of goodness that they assumed it was beyond their reach. The very idea of always, all the day, abiding in Jesus was too high—something they might attain to after a life of holiness and growth, but certainly not what an immature beginner was to start with.

They did not know how, when Jesus said, "My yoke is easy," He spoke the truth; how it is actually *the yoke* which gives the rest, because the moment the soul yields itself to obey, the Lord himself gives the strength and joy to do it. They did not notice how when He said, "Learn from Me," He added, "for I am gentle and lowly in heart," to assure them that His gentleness would meet their every need and sustain them as a mother upholds her weakest child. They did not know that when He said, "Abide in Me," He only asked that His followers surrender to Him; His almighty love would keep and bless them. And so, as some fell short of full consecration, they failed because they did not fully trust. These two, consecration and faith, are the essential elements of the Christian life—the giving up of all to Jesus, the receiving of all from Jesus. They are implied in each other; they are united in one word: *surrender*. A full surrender is to obey as well as to trust, to trust as well as to obey.

With such misunderstanding at the outset, it is no wonder that the disciple's life is often not filled with as much joy or strength as had been hoped. In some things you were led into sin without knowing it, because you had not learned how wholly Jesus wanted to rule you and how you could not remain righteous for a moment unless you had Him very near you. In other things you knew what sin was, but did not have the power to conquer, because you did not know or believe how entirely Jesus would keep and help you. Either way, it was not long before the bright joy of your first love was lost, and your path, instead of being like the "path of the righteous . . . shining ever brighter till the full light of day" (Proverbs 4:18 NIV), became like Israel's wandering in the desert, ever on the way, never very far, and yet always coming short of the promised rest. Weary soul, come and learn this day the lesson that there is a spot where safety and victory, peace and rest, are always sure. That place, which is the heart of Jesus, is always open to you.

But, sadly, I hear someone say it is just this abiding in Jesus, always bearing His yoke to learn from Him, that is so difficult, and the very effort to attain to this often disturbs my rest even more than sin or the world. What a mistake it is to speak like this, yet how often the words are heard! We must ask ourselves, does it make the traveler even wearier to rest in the house or on the bed where he seeks relief from his fatigue? Or is it work to a little child to rest in his mother's arms? Is it not the house that keeps the traveler within its shelter? Do not the arms of the mother sustain and keep the little one? And so it is with Jesus.

The soul has only to yield itself to Him, to be still and to rest in the confidence that His love has undertaken, and that His faithfulness will perform, the work of keeping it safe. It is because the blessing is so great that our frail hearts cannot rise to grasp it; it is as if we cannot believe that Christ, the Almighty One, will actually teach and keep us all day. And yet this is just what He has promised, for without this He cannot really give us rest. It is His own work to keep us abiding when we yield ourselves to Him. We must risk casting ourselves into the arms of His love, and so abandon ourselves to His blessed keeping. It is not the yoke, but resistance to the yoke, that makes the difficulty; wholehearted surrender to Jesus, our Master and our Keeper, is what finds and secures our rest.

Come, my fellow believers, and let us this very day begin to accept the word of Jesus in all its simplicity. It is a distinct command to "Take My yoke . . . and learn from Me"; "Abide in Me." A command has to be obeyed. The obedient scholar asks no questions about possibilities or results; he accepts every order in the confidence that his teacher has provided for all that is needed. The power and the perseverance to abide in His rest, and the blessing in abiding, belongs to the Savior: 'tis mine to obey, 'tis His to provide. Let us this day in immediate obedience accept the command, and answer boldly, "Savior, I abide in you. At your bidding I take your yoke upon me; I undertake the duty without delay; I abide in you." May each time we fail only give new urgency to the command, and teach us to listen more earnestly than ever until the Spirit gives us the voice of Jesus saying with love and authority the words that inspire both hope and obedience: "Child, abide in Me." That word, heard as coming from Jesus himself, will be an end to all doubting—a divine promise of what will surely be granted. And with ever-increasing simplicity its meaning will be interpreted. Abiding in Jesus is nothing but the giving up of oneself to be ruled, taught, and led, enabling the disciple to rest in the arms of Everlasting Love.

What a blessed rest it is! The fruit, the foretaste, and the fellowship of God's own rest are found by them who have come to Jesus to abide in Him. It is the peace of God, the great calm of the eternal world, that passes all understanding and that keeps the heart and mind. With this grace secured, we have strength for every duty, courage for every struggle, a blessing in every cross, and the joy of life eternal in death itself.

O my Savior, if ever my heart should doubt or fear again, as if the blessing were too great to expect, or too high to attain, let me hear your voice, which alone can create faith and obedience in me: "Abide in Me"; "Take My yoke upon you and learn from Me; you will find rest for your souls."

Trusting Him to Keep You

*I press on to take hold of that for which
Christ Jesus took hold of me.*

Philippians 3:12 (NIV)

More than one admits that it is a sacred duty and a blessed privilege to abide in Christ but shrinks back continually before the question: Is it possible, a life of unbroken fellowship with the Savior? Eminent Christians, to whom special opportunities of cultivating this grace have been granted, may attain to it; but for the large majority of disciples whose lives are so fully occupied with the everyday concerns of this life, it cannot be expected. The more they hear of this life, the deeper their sense of its glory and blessing, and there is nothing they would not sacrifice to be made partakers of it. But they feel they are too weak, too unfaithful; they are sure they can never attain it.

How little such dear souls know about this life. They don't realize that abiding in Christ is meant for the weak and is beautifully suited to their frailty. It is not the doing of some great thing and does not demand that we first lead a very holy and devoted life. No, it is simply weakness entrusting itself to a Mighty One to be kept, the unfaithful one casting itself on One who is altogether trustworthy and true. Abiding in Him is not a work that we have to do as the condition for enjoying His salvation, but rather a consenting to let Him do all for us, in us, and through us. It is a work He does for us as the fruit and the power of His redeeming love. Our part is simply to yield, to trust, and to wait for what He has promised to perform.

It is this quiet expectation and confidence, resting on the word of Christ that *in Him* there is an abiding place prepared, which is so sadly lacking among Christians. For when He says, "Abide in Me," He offers himself, the Keeper of Israel that neither slumbers nor sleeps (Psalm 121:4), with all His power and love, as *the living home of the soul,* where the mighty influences of His grace will be stronger to keep than all of the disciples' tendencies to be led astray. The idea so many Christians have of grace is this: that their conversion and pardon are God's work, but now, in gratitude to God, it is their work to live as Christians and follow Jesus. There is always the thought of a work that has to be done, and even though they pray for help, still the work is theirs. They fail continually and become hopeless; and their despondency only increases their feelings of helplessness.

No, wandering one; as it was Jesus who drew you when He said, "Come," so it is Jesus who keeps you when He says, "Abide." The grace to come and the grace to abide are both from Him alone. That word *come*—heard, meditated on, accepted—was the cord of love that drew you close; the word *abide* is the band with which He holds you fast and binds you to himself. Let the soul take time to listen to the voice of Jesus. "*In Me*," He says, "is your place—in my almighty arms. It is I, the One who loves you so, who now speaks 'Abide in Me'; surely you can trust Me." The voice of Jesus entering and dwelling in the soul draws us to respond: "Yes, Savior, *in you* I can, I will abide."

"*Abide in Me*": These words are no law of Moses, demanding from the sinful what they cannot perform. They are the command of love, which is only a promise in a different shape. Think of this until all feeling of burden, fear, and despair pass away, and the first thought that comes as you hear of abiding in Jesus is one of bright and joyous hope: It is for me; I know I will enjoy it. You are not under the law, with its demanding *Do*, but under grace, with its blessed *Believe* what Christ will do for you. And if the question is asked, "But surely there is something for us to do," the answer is, "Our doing and working are but the fruit of Christ's work in us." It is when the soul becomes utterly passive, looking and resting on what Christ is to do, that its energies are stirred to their highest activity, and we work most effectively because we know that He works in us. It is as we see in the words "in Me" the mighty energies of love reaching out after us to have us and to hold us, that all the strength of our will is awakened to abide in Him.

This connection between Christ's work and our work is beautifully expressed in the words of Paul: "I press on, to *take hold of* that for which Christ Jesus *took hold* of me." It was because he knew that the mighty and the faithful One had grasped him with the glorious purpose of making him one with Christ that he did his utmost to grasp the glorious prize. The faith, the experience, the full assurance, "Christ Jesus took hold of me," gave him the courage and the strength to press on and take hold of that for which he was taken. Each new insight of the great end for which Christ had taken him spurred him on to aim for nothing less.

Paul's expression, and its application to the Christian life, can be best understood if we think of a father helping his child to climb the side of some steep precipice. The father stands above and has taken the son by the hand to help him on. He points him to the spot on which he will help him to plant his feet as he leaps upward. The leap would be too high and dangerous for the child alone, but the father's hand is his trust and he leaps to get hold of the point for which his father has taken hold of him. It is the father's strength that secures him and lifts him up, and so urges him to use his utmost strength.

Such is the relationship between Christ and you, O weak and trembling believer! Fix your eyes first on the *that* for which He has taken hold of you. It is nothing less than a life of abiding, unbroken fellowship with himself to which He is seeking to lift you up. All that you have already received—pardon and peace, the Spirit and His grace—are but preliminary to this. And all that you see promised to you in the future—holiness and fruitfulness and glory everlasting—are but its natural outcome. *Union with himself,* and so with the Father, is His highest object. Fix your eye on this, and gaze until it stands out before you clear and unmistakable: Christ's aim is to have me abiding in Him.

Then let the second thought enter your heart: *For this Christ Jesus took hold of me.* His almighty power has taken hold of me and offers now to lift me up to where He would have me. Fix your eyes on Christ. Gaze on the love that shines in those eyes and that asks whether you can trust Him, who sought, found, and brought you near, now to keep you. Gaze on that arm of power, and say whether you have reason enough to be assured that He is indeed able to keep you abiding in Him.

And as you think of the spot He points to—the blessed *that* for which He laid hold of you—and keep your gaze fixed on Him holding you and waiting to lift you up, begin at once to say, "O my Jesus, if you bid me, and if you will indeed lift me up and keep me there, I will venture. Trembling, but trusting, I will say, 'Jesus, I do abide in you.'"

My beloved fellow believers, go, and take time alone with Jesus, and say this to Him. I do not speak to you about abiding in Him for the mere sake of calling forth a pleasing religious sentiment. God's truth must be acted on at once. Yield yourself this very day to the blessed Savior by surrendering the one thing He asks of you: Give up yourself to abide in Him. He himself will work it in you. You can trust Him to keep you trusting and abiding.

And if ever doubts arise, or the bitter experience of failure tempts you to despair, just remember where Paul found His strength: "Christ Jesus took hold of me." In that assurance you have a fountain of strength. From that you can look up to where He has set His heart and set yours there too. From that truth you can gather confidence that the good work He began in you He will carry on to completion (Philippians 1:6). And in that confidence you will gather courage day by day to say, "I press on, to take hold of that for which Christ Jesus took hold of me." It is because Jesus has taken hold of me, and because Jesus keeps me, that I dare to say: "Savior, I abide in you."

As the Branch in the Vine

I am the vine, you are the branches.

John 15:5

It was in connection with the parable of the Vine that our Lord first used the expression "Abide in Me." That parable, so simple and yet so rich in its teaching, gives us the best and most complete illustration of the meaning of our Lord's command and the union to which He invites us.

The parable teaches us *the nature* of that union. The connection between the vine and the branch is a living one. No external, temporary union is described here, and no work of man can make it happen. The branch, whether an original or an engrafted one, is the Creator's own work; the life, the sap, the fatness, and the fruitfulness of the branch are only possible because of its attachment to the vine. And so it is with the believer too. His union with his Lord is no work of human wisdom or human will, but an act of God, by which the closest and most complete life-union possible is forged between the

Son of God and the sinner. "God has sent forth the Spirit of His Son into your hearts" (Galatians 4:6). The same Spirit that dwelt and still dwells in the Son becomes the life of the believer; in the unity of that one Spirit, and the fellowship of the same life that is in Christ, he is one with Him. As between the vine and branch, it is a life-union that makes them one.

The parable teaches us the *completeness* of the union. So close is the union between the vine and the branch, that each is nothing without the other, each is wholly and only for the other.

Without the vine the branch can do nothing. To the vine it owes its right of place in the vineyard, its life and its fruitfulness. And so the Lord says, "Without Me you can do nothing." The believer can each day be pleasing to God only in that which he does through the power of Christ dwelling in him. The daily filling of the life-sap of the Holy Spirit is his only power to bring forth fruit. He lives in Him alone and is for each moment dependent on Him alone.

Without the branch the vine can also do nothing. A vine without branches can bear no fruit. No less indispensable than the vine to the branch is the branch to the vine. Such is the wonderful condescension of the grace of Jesus; just as His people are dependent on Him, He has made himself dependent on them. Without His disciples He cannot dispense His blessing to the world. I know it seems incredible, but it is true! This is God's own doing, giving such high honor to those He has called His redeemed ones, designing it so that as indispensable as He is to them in acquiring fruit and winning heaven, so indispensable are they to Him on earth, that through them His fruit may be found. Believers, meditate on this until your soul bows to

This is hard to grasp

worship in the presence of the mystery of the perfect union between Christ and the believer.

There is more: As neither vine nor branch is anything *without* the other, so is neither anything except *for* the other. *All the vine possesses belongs to the branches.* The vine does not gather from the soil its fatness and its sweetness for itself; all it has is at the disposal of the branches. As it is the parent, so it is the servant of the branches. How completely Jesus, to whom we owe our life, gives himself for us and to us: "The glory which You gave Me I have given them" (John 17:22); "He who believes in Me, the works that I do he will do also; and greater works than these he will do, because I go to My Father" (John 14:12). All His fullness and all His riches are for you, as His believer; for the vine does not live for itself, or keep anything for itself, but exists only for the branches. All that Jesus is in heaven, He is for us. He has no interest there separate from ours; as our representative He stands before the Father on our behalf.

And all the branch possesses belongs to the vine. The branch does not exist for itself, but to bear fruit that can proclaim the excellence of the vine; it has no reason to exist except to be of service to the vine. What a glorious image this is of the calling of the believer; the entirety of his consecration is only for service to his Lord. As Jesus gives himself so completely over to him, he feels himself urged to be wholly his Lord's. Every power of his being, every moment of his life, every thought and feeling belong to Jesus, that from Him and for Him he may bring forth fruit. As he realizes what the vine is to the branch, and what the branch is meant to be to the vine, he feels that he has but one thing to think of and to live for: the will, the glory, the work, the kingdom of his blessed Lord—the bringing forth of fruit to the glory of His name.

The parable also teaches us *the object* of the union. The branches are for *fruit* and *fruit alone.* "Every branch in Me that does not bear fruit He takes away." The branch needs leaves for the maintenance of its own life and the perfection of its fruit; the fruit it bears is to be given away to those around it. As the believer enters into his calling as a branch, he sees that he has to forget himself and to live entirely for others. To love them, to seek for them, and to save them, this is why Jesus came. For this purpose every branch on the Vine—as well as the Vine—must live. *It is for fruit, much fruit,* that the Father has made us one with Jesus.

Wondrous parable of the Vine—unveiling the mysteries of divine love, of the heavenly life, of the world of the Spirit—how little have I understood you! Jesus the living Vine in heaven, and I the living branch on earth—how profound are the implications of this revelation. I have scarcely grasped how great my need is, but also how perfect is my claim to all His fullness! How little have I understood how great His need is, but also how perfect is His claim to my emptiness! Let me, in its beautiful light, study the wondrous union between Jesus and His people until it becomes to me the guide into full communion with my beloved Lord. Let me listen and believe, until my whole being cries out, "Jesus is indeed to me the True Vine, bearing me, nourishing me, supplying me, using me, and filling me to the full to make me bring forth fruit abundantly." Then I will not be afraid to say, "I am indeed a branch of Jesus, the True Vine, abiding in Him, resting on Him, waiting for Him, serving Him, and living so that through me, too, He may exhibit the riches of His grace, and give His fruit to a dying world."

It is when we try to understand the meaning of the parable that the blessed command spoken in connection with it will come home to us in its true power. The thought of what the vine is to the branch, and Jesus to the believer, will give new power to the words "Abide in Me!" It will be as if He says, "Think, believer, how completely I belong to you. I have joined myself inseparably to you; all the fullness and fatness of the Vine are yours. It is My desire and My honor to make you a fruitful branch; only *Abide in Me.* You are weak, but I am strong; you are poor, but I am rich. Only abide in Me; yield yourself wholly to My teaching and rule; simply trust My love, My grace, and My promises. Only believe; I am wholly yours; I am the Vine, you are the branch. Abide in Me."

What is my response to such a revelation? Should I continue to hesitate, or withhold consent? Or should I—instead of only thinking about how hard and how difficult it is to live like a branch of the True Vine, because I thought of it as something I had to accomplish—now begin to look upon it as the most blessed and joyful thing under heaven? Should I not believe that, now that I am in Him, He himself will keep me and enable me to abide? On my part, abiding is nothing but the acceptance of my position, the consent to be kept there, the surrender of faith to the strong Vine to hold the frail branch. Yes, I will, I do abide in you, blessed Lord Jesus.

O Savior, how unspeakable is your love! "Such knowledge is too wonderful for me, too lofty for me to attain" (Psalm 139:6 NIV). I can only yield myself to your love with the prayer that, day by day, you would reveal to me the precious mysteries of such knowledge and so encourage and strengthen me to do what my heart longs to do indeed—ever, only, wholly to abide in you.

It Is As You Came to Him, by Faith

As you have therefore received Christ Jesus the Lord, so walk in Him, rooted and built up in Him and established in the faith, as you have been taught, abounding in it with thanksgiving.

Colossians 2:6–7

In these words the apostle teaches us an important lesson, that it is not only by faith that we first come to Christ and are united to Him but also by faith that we are to be rooted and established in our union with Christ. Faith is essential not only for the commencement, but also for the progress of the spiritual life. Abiding in Jesus can only be by faith.

There are sincere Christians who do not understand this; or, if they admit it in theory, they fail to realize its application in practice. They are very zealous for a free gospel in which our first acceptance of Christ and justification is by faith alone. But after this they think everything depends on our diligence and faithfulness. While most firmly grasp the truth "The sinner is justified by faith" (Galatians 2:16), they rarely find a place for the larger truth, "The just shall *live* by faith" (Romans 1:17). They have not understood what a perfect Savior Jesus is, and how He will each day do for the sinner just as much as He did the first day he came to Him. They do not know that the life of grace is always and only a life of faith, and that in the relationship to Jesus the one daily and unceasing duty of the disciple is *to believe*, because believing is the one channel through which divine grace and strength flow out into the heart of His people.

The old nature of the believer remains evil and sinful to the last; it is only as he daily comes, empty and helpless, to his Savior to receive His life and strength, that he can bring forth fruits of righteousness to the glory of God. Therefore it is: "*As* you have therefore received Christ Jesus the Lord, so walk *in Him*, rooted and built up *in Him* and established *in the faith*, as you have been taught, abounding in it with thanksgiving." As you came to Jesus, so abide in Him, by faith.

And if you would know how faith is to be exercised in this abiding, how you can be rooted more deeply and firmly in Him, you will need to look back to the time when you first received Him. You remember well the obstacles that appeared to be in the way of your believing. There was first your corruption and guilt; it appeared impossible that the promise of pardon and love could be for a sinner like you. Then there was the sense of weakness and death: You did not feel the power necessary for the surrender and the trust to which you were called. And then there was the future: You did not dare to imagine you could be a disciple of Jesus while you felt so unable to stand. You were sure you would quickly revert to unfaithfulness and fall. These difficulties were like mountains in your way. And how were they removed? Simply by the word of God. That word compelled you to believe that despite guilt in the past, weakness in the present, and unfaithfulness in the future, the promise was sure that Jesus would accept you and save you. On that word you ventured to come, and were not deceived: You found that Jesus did indeed accept and save you.

Now apply this, your experience in coming to Jesus, to abiding in Him. Now, as then, the temptations to keep you from believing are many. When you think of your sins since you became a disciple, your heart is cast down with shame, and it looks as if it were too much to expect that Jesus would indeed receive you into perfect intimacy and the full enjoyment of His holy love. When you think how utterly, in times past, you have failed to keep the most sacred vows, the consciousness of present weakness makes you tremble at the very idea of answering the Savior's command with the promise "Lord, from now on I will abide in you." And when you set before yourself the life of love and joy, of holiness and fruitfulness, which in the future are to flow from abiding in Him, it is as if it only serves to make you still more hopeless; you are sure you can never attain to it. You know yourself too well. There is no use expecting it, only to be disappointed; a life fully and wholly abiding in Jesus is not for you.

Oh, that you would learn a lesson from the time of your first coming to the Savior! Remember, dear one, how you were then led—contrary to all that your experience, your feelings, and even your sober judgment said—to take Jesus at His word, and how you were not disappointed. He did receive you, and pardon you; He did love you, and save you. And if He did this for you when you were an enemy and a stranger, now that you are His own, will He not much more fulfill His promise? (See

Romans 5:10.) Oh, that you would come and begin simply to listen to His word, and to ask only one question: Does He really mean that I can abide in Him? The answer His word gives is so simple and so sure: By His almighty grace you are now *in Him*; that same almighty grace will indeed enable you to abide in Him. By faith you became a partaker of the initial grace; by that same faith you can enjoy the continuous grace of abiding in Him.

And if you ask what exactly it is that you now have to believe that you may abide in Him, the answer is not difficult. Believe first of all what He says: "I am the Vine." The safety and the fruitfulness of the branch depend upon the strength of the vine. Do not think so much of yourself as a branch, nor of the abiding as your duty, until you have first had your soul filled with faith in what Christ as the Vine is. *He really will be to you all that a vine can be*—holding you fast, nourishing you, and making himself responsible every moment for your growth and your fruit. Take time to know, set yourself to believe heartily: My Vine, on whom I can depend for all I need, is Christ. A large, strong vine bears a weak branch and holds it more than the branch holds the vine. Ask the Father by the Holy Spirit to reveal to you what a glorious, loving, mighty Christ this is, in whom you have your place and your life; it is *faith in what Christ is*, more than anything else, that will keep you abiding in Him. A soul filled with large thoughts of the Vine will be a strong branch and will abide confidently in Him. Turn your attention to Jesus and exercise your faith in Him as the True Vine.

And then, when Faith can confidently say, "He is my Vine," let it further say, "I am His branch, I am in Him." I speak to those who say they are Christ's disciples, and on them I cannot too earnestly press the importance of exercising their faith in saying, "I am in Him." It makes abiding so simple. If I realize clearly as I meditate: Now I am in Him, I see at once that there is nothing lacking but my consent to be what He has made me, to remain where He has placed me. *I am in Christ*: This simple thought, carefully, prayerfully, believingly uttered, removes the fear that there is yet some great attainment to be reached. No, *I am in Christ*, my blessed Savior. His love has prepared a home for me with himself. When He says, "Abide in My love," His power has undertaken to open the door and to keep me in this home He has prepared for me, if I will but consent. *I am in Christ*: now all I need to say is, "Savior, I thank you for this wondrous grace. I consent; I yield myself to your gracious keeping; I do abide in you."

It is astonishing how such faith will work out all that is further implied in abiding in Christ. There is in the Christian life a great need for watchfulness and prayer, of self-denial, obedience, and diligence. But "all things are possible to him who believes" (Mark 9:23). "This is the victory that has overcome the world—our faith"(1 John 5:4). It is faith that continually closes its eyes to the weakness of the creature, and finds its joy in the sufficiency of an almighty Savior, that makes the soul strong and glad. It gives itself up to be led by the Holy Spirit into an ever-deeper appreciation of that wonderful Savior given to us by God. This faith follows the leading of the Spirit from page to page of the blessed Word with the one desire to take each revelation of what Jesus is and what He promises as its nourishment and its life. In accordance with the promise "If what you have heard from the beginning abides in you, you also will abide in the Son and in the Father" (1 John 2:24), you will live "by every word that proceeds out of the mouth of God" (Matthew 4:4). And so the Word makes us strong with the strength of God, to enable us to abide in Christ.

Believer, if you would abide in Christ: only believe. Believe always; believe now. Bow even now before your Lord, and say to Him in childlike faith that, because He is your Vine and you are His branch, you will this day abide in Him.

Note: It is perhaps necessary to say, for the sake of young or doubting Christians, that there is something more necessary than the effort to exercise faith in each separate promise that is brought to our attention. What is of even greater importance is the cultivation of a trustful disposition toward God, the habit of always thinking of Him, of His ways and His works, with confidence and hope. In such soil alone can individual promises take root and grow.

God Has United You to Himself

*Of Him [God] you are in Christ Jesus, who became for us
wisdom from God—and righteousness and
sanctification and redemption.*

1 Corinthians 1:30

My Father is the vinedresser.

John 15:1

"You are in Christ Jesus." The believers at Corinth were still weak and carnal, only babes in Christ. And yet Paul wanted them, at the outset of his teaching, to know distinctly that they were in Christ Jesus. The whole Christian life depends on the clear consciousness of our position in Christ. Most essential to abiding in Christ is the daily renewal of our faith's assurance, "I am in Christ Jesus." All fruitful preaching to believers must begin with: "You are in Christ Jesus."

But the apostle has an additional thought, of almost greater importance: "Of God are you in Christ Jesus." He would have us not only remember our union to Christ but also, more particularly, that it is not our own doing, but the work of God himself. As the Holy Spirit teaches us to realize this, we will see what a source of assurance and strength it is to us. If it is of God alone that I am in Christ, then God himself, the Infinite One, becomes my security for all I need or desire in seeking to abide in Christ.

Let me try to explain what it means, this wonderful truth "Of God in Christ." In becoming one with Christ, there is a work God does and a work we have to do. God does His work by moving us to do our work. The work of God is hidden and silent; what we do is something distinct and tangible. Conversion and faith along with prayer and obedience are conscious acts of which we can give a clear account, while the spiritual awakening and strengthening that come from above are secret and beyond the reach of human sight. So often when the believer tries to say, "I am in Christ Jesus," he looks more to the work *he* has done than to that wondrous secret work of God, which united him to Christ. This is to be expected at the beginning of the Christian course. "I know that I have believed," is a valid testimony. But it is important that the mind be led to see that at the back of our turning, believing, and accepting of Christ, God's almighty power was doing its work of inspiring our will, taking possession of us, and carrying out its own purpose of love in planting us into Christ Jesus. As the believer understands the divine side of the work of salvation, he will learn to praise and to worship with new enthusiasm and to rejoice more than ever in his salvation. At each step he reviews, the song will come, "This is the Lord's doing"— Divine Omnipotence working out what Eternal Love devised. "Of God I am in Christ Jesus."

The words will lead him even further and higher, and to the very depths of eternity. "And *those* he predestined, he also called" (Romans 8:30 NIV). The calling in time is the manifestation of God's purpose in eternity. For before the world came into existence, God had His eyes of sovereign love fixed on you in the election of grace and had chosen you in Christ. That you know you are in Christ is the key to understanding the full meaning of this word: "Of God I am in Christ Jesus." With the prophet, your language will be, "The Lord has appeared to us in the past, saying: 'I have loved you with an everlasting love, I have drawn you with loving-kindness'" (Jeremiah 31:3 NIV). And you will see your own salvation as a part of that "mystery of his will according to his good pleasure, which he purposed in Christ" (Ephesians 1:9 NIV) and join with the whole church as they say, "In him we were also chosen, having been predestined according to the plan of him who works out everything in conformity with the purpose of his will" (Ephesians 1:11 NIV). Nothing will exalt free grace more, and make man bow very low before it, than this knowledge of the mystery of His will: "Of God in Christ."

It is easy to see what a great influence this truth will exert on the believer who seeks to abide in Christ. What a sure standing-ground it gives him, as he rests his right to Christ and all His fullness on nothing less than the Father's own purpose and work! We have thought of Christ as the Vine, and the believer as the branch; let us not forget that other precious word, "My Father is the vinedresser." The Savior said, "Every plant which My heavenly Father has not planted will be uprooted" (Matthew 15:13); but every branch grafted by Him into the True Vine will never be plucked out of His hand (John 10:28). As it was the Father to whom Christ owed all He was, and in whom He had all His strength and His life as the Vine, so to the Father the believer owes his place and his security in Christ. It is with the same love and delight with which the Father watched over the beloved Son that God the Father now watches over every member of His body, every one who is in Christ Jesus.

What confident trust this faith inspires—not only in being kept in safety to the end, but also in being able to fulfill in every point the object for which I have been united to Christ. The branch is as much in the keeping of the vinedresser as is the vine. God's honor is as much at stake in the well-being and growth of the branch as it is in that of the vine. The God who chose Christ to be the Vine made Him thoroughly fit for the work He had to perform. The God who has chosen me and planted me in Christ as a branch has ensured (if I will let Him, by yielding myself to Him) that I will in every way be worthy of Jesus Christ. Oh, to fully realize this truth! What confidence and urgency it would give to my prayer to the God and Father of Jesus Christ! How it would deepen my sense of dependence and enable me to see that continual praying is the one need of my life—an unceasing waiting, moment by moment, on the God who has united me to Christ, to perfect His own divine work in me.

And what a motive this would be for the highest activity in the maintenance of a fruitful branch-life! Motives are mighty powers; it is of infinite importance that we keep them high and clear. Here surely is the highest motive of all: "We are His (God's) workmanship, created in Christ Jesus for good works" (Ephesians 2:10). We have been grafted by Him into Christ, to bring forth much fruit. Whatever God creates is exquisitely suited to its end. He created the sun to give light, and how perfectly it does its work! He created the eye to see, and how beautifully it fulfills its object! And He created the new man to do good works; can we affirm that our new nature is also perfectly formed for its purpose?

Of God I am in Christ: created anew, made a branch of the Vine, and made for bearing fruit. Oh, that believers would stop looking at their old nature so much, and complaining of their weakness, as if God called them for what they were unsuited! How much better for them to believingly and joyfully accept the wondrous revelation of how God, in uniting them to Christ, has made himself responsible for their spiritual growth and fruitfulness! Then all hesitancy and laziness would disappear, and under the influence of this mighty motive—faith in the faithfulness of Him of whom they are in Christ—their whole nature would arise to accept and fulfill their glorious destiny!

It is the same God of whom Christ is made all that He is for us, of whom we also are in Christ and will be made what we must be to Him. Take time to meditate and to worship, until the light that comes from the throne of God has shone into you, and you have seen your union to Christ as the work of His almighty Father. Take time, day after day, in your whole Christian walk, with all its claims, duties, needs, and desires, and let God be everything. See Jesus, as He speaks to you, "Abide in Me," pointing upward and saying, "My Father is the vine-dresser. *Of Him* you are in Me, *through Him* you abide in Me, and *to Him* and to His glory shall be the fruit you bear." And let your answer be, Amen, Lord! So be it. From eternity Christ and I were ordained for each other; inseparably we belong to each other. It is God's will for me to abide in Christ. It is of God I am in Christ Jesus.

He Is Your Wisdom

Of Him (God) you are in Christ Jesus, who became for us
WISDOM from God—and righteousness and
sanctification and redemption.

1 Corinthians 1:30

Jesus Christ is not only Priest to purchase, and King to secure, but also Prophet to reveal to us the salvation that God prepared for them who love Him. Just as at creation the light was first called into existence, that in it all God's other works might have their life and beauty, so in our text wisdom is mentioned first as the treasury in which are found the three precious gifts that follow. The life is the light of man (John 1:4); in revealing this to us, and enabling us to see the glory of God in His own face, Christ makes us partakers of eternal life. It was by the Tree of Knowledge that sin came; it is through the knowledge that Christ gives that salvation comes. He is made of God wisdom for us. *In Him* are hidden all the treasures of wisdom and knowledge (Colossians 2:3).

And of God you are *in Him*, and only have to abide in Him to be made partaker of these treasures of wisdom. *In Him* you are, and *in Him* the wisdom is; dwelling in Him, you dwell in the very fountain of all light; abiding in Him, you have Christ, the wisdom of God, leading your whole spiritual life. He is ready to communicate, in the form of knowledge, just as much as is needful for you to know. Christ is made to us wisdom: You are in Christ.

It is this connection between what Christ has been made for us, and how we have it only as we are in Him, that we need to understand better. The blessings prepared for us in Christ cannot be obtained as special gifts in answer to prayer *apart from abiding in Him.* The answer to each prayer must come in a closer union and deeper abiding in Him; in Him—the unspeakable gift—all other gifts are treasured up, including the gifts of wisdom and knowledge.

How often have you longed for wisdom and spiritual understanding that you might *know God* better, whom to know is life eternal? Abide in Jesus: Your life in Him will lead you to that fellowship with God in which the only true knowledge of God can be found. You may not be able to grasp it with understanding, or to express it in words; but the knowledge that is deeper than thoughts or words will be given—the knowing of God that comes from being known of Him. "We preach Christ crucified . . . to those who are called . . . Christ the power of God and the wisdom of God" (1 Corinthians 1:23–24).

Would you count all things but loss for the excellency of the *knowledge of Jesus Christ* your Lord (Philippians 3:8)? Then abide in Jesus, and be found in Him. You will know Him in the power of His resurrection and the fellowship of His sufferings (Philippians 3:10). Following Him, you will not walk in darkness, but will have the light of life (John 8:12). It is only when

God shines into the heart, and Christ Jesus dwells there, that the light of the knowledge of God in the face of Christ can be seen.

Would you understand His blessed *work*, as He brings it to pass on earth or works it from heaven by His Spirit? Would you know how Christ has become our righteousness, our sanctification, and our redemption? It is by bringing, revealing, and communicating these that He is made to us wisdom from God. There are a thousand questions that at times come up, and the attempt to answer them sometimes becomes a burden. It is because you have forgotten you are in Christ, whom God has made to be your wisdom. Let it be your first aim to abide in Him in focused, fervent devotion of heart; when the heart and the life are right, rooted in Christ, knowledge will come in the measure we need. Without such abiding in Christ, knowledge does not really profit, but can actually be hurtful.

The soul may satisfy itself with thoughts that are but the forms and images of truth, without receiving the truth itself in its power. God's way is to first give us, even though it is but as a seed, the thing itself, the life and the power, and then comes the knowledge. Man seeks the knowledge first and often never gets beyond it. God gives us Christ, and in Him are *hidden* the treasures of wisdom and knowledge. Let us be content to possess Christ, to dwell in Him, to make Him our life. Only in a deeper searching into Him will we find the knowledge we desire. Such knowledge is life indeed.

Therefore, believer, abide in Jesus as your wisdom, and confidently expect from Him whatever teaching you may need for living your life to the glory of the Father. In all that concerns your *spiritual life*, abide in Jesus as your wisdom. The life you have in Christ is a thing of infinite sacredness, far too high and holy for you to naturally know how to act it out. He alone can guide you, as by a secret spiritual instinct, to know what will help and what will hinder your inner life, and enable you to abide in Him.

Do not think of it as a mystery or a difficulty you must solve. In whatever questions come up about abiding perfectly in Him at all times, and of obtaining all the blessing that comes from abiding, always remember: He knows, all is perfectly clear to Him, and He is your wisdom. Just as much as you need to know, and are capable of understanding, will be communicated, *if you only trust Him.* Never think of the riches of wisdom and knowledge hidden in Jesus as treasures without a key, or of your way as a path without a light. Jesus your wisdom is guiding you in the right way, even when you do not see it.

In all your meditations with the *blessed Word*, remember the same truth: Abide in Jesus, your wisdom. Study as much as you can to know the written Word; but study even more to know the living Word, in whom you are of God. Jesus, the wisdom of God, is only known by a life of implicit confidence and obedience. The words He speaks are spirit and life to those *who live in Him.* Therefore, each time you read, or hear, or meditate upon the Word, be careful to assume your true position. Realize first your oneness with Him who is the wisdom of God; know yourself to be under His direct and special training; go to the Word abiding in Him, the very fountain of divine light. *In His light* you can and will see light.

In all *your daily life*, its ways and its work, abide in Jesus as your wisdom. Your body and your daily life share in the great salvation: In Christ, the wisdom of God, provision has been made for their guidance too. Your body is His temple, your daily life the sphere for glorifying Him. It is a matter of deep interest to Him that all your earthly concerns be guided rightly. Trust His sympathy, believe His love, and wait for His guidance—it will be given. Abiding in Him, the mind will be calm and free from distraction, judgment will be clear as the light of heaven shines on earthly things, and your prayer for wisdom, like Solomon's, will be fulfilled "exceedingly abundantly above all that (you) ask or think" (Ephesians 3:20).

And so, especially in any *work* you do for God, abide in Jesus as your wisdom. Remember, we are "created in Christ Jesus for good works, which God has prepared beforehand that we should walk in them" (Ephesians 2:10). Put away any fears or doubts that you will not know exactly what these works are. In Christ we are created for them; He will show us what they are and how to do them. Cultivate the habit of rejoicing in the assurance that the God of divine wisdom is guiding you, even where you do not yet see the way.

All that you can wish to know is perfectly clear to Him. As Man, our Mediator, He has access to the counsels of Deity, to the secrets of Providence, in your interest and on your behalf. If you will but trust Him fully, and abide in Him entirely, you can be confident of having unerring guidance.

Yes, abide in Jesus as your wisdom. Seek to maintain the spirit of waiting and dependence, the spirit that always seeks to learn and moves only as the heavenly light leads on. Withdraw yourself from all needless distraction, close your ears to the voices of the world, and be as a docile learner, always listening for the heavenly wisdom the Master has to teach. Surrender all your own wisdom; seek a deep conviction of the utter blindness of the natural understanding in the things of God; and wait for Jesus to teach and to guide in all you believe and do. Remember that His teaching and guidance do not come outside you: It is by *His life in us* that Divine Wisdom does His work.

Retire frequently with Him into the inner chamber of the heart, where the gentle voice of the Spirit is only heard if all is still. Hang on with unshaken confidence, even in the midst of darkness and apparent desertion, to His own assurance that He is the light and the leader of His own. And live, above all, day by day in the blessed truth that, as He himself, the living Christ Jesus, is your wisdom, your first and last care must be this alone—to abide in Him. Abiding in Him, His wisdom will come to you as the spontaneous outflow of a life rooted in Him. I am, I abide, in Christ, who was *made to us* wisdom from God; wisdom will be given to me.

IHCTHUS

He Is Your Righteousness

*Of Him (God) you are in Christ Jesus, who became for us
wisdom from God—and RIGHTEOUSNESS and
sanctification and redemption.*

1 Corinthians 1:30

The first of the great blessings that Christ our wisdom reveals to us as prepared in himself, is *righteousness*. It is not difficult to see why this must be first.

There can be no real prosperity or progress in a nation, a home, or a soul without peace. As not even a machine can do its work unless it is at rest, secured on a good foundation, so quietness and assurance are indispensable to our moral and spiritual well-being. Sin disturbed all our relationships; we were out of harmony with ourselves, with others, and with God. The first requirement of a salvation that would bring blessing to us is peace. And peace can only come with righteousness. Peace can reign only where everything is as God would have it, in God's order and in harmony with His will. Jesus Christ came to restore peace on earth, and peace in the soul, by restoring righteousness. Because He is Melchizedek, King of righteousness, He reigns as King of Salem, King of peace (Hebrews 7:2). In this, He fulfills the promise the prophets held out: "A king will reign in righteousness ... the fruit of righteousness will be peace; the effect of righteousness will be quietness and confidence forever" (Isaiah 32:1, 17 NIV). God has made Christ to be righteousness for us; because of God we are in Him as our righteousness. In fact, we are made the righteousness of God in Him (2 Corinthians 5:21). Let us try to understand what this means.

When the sinner is first led to trust in Christ for salvation, he, as a rule, looks more to Christ's work than His person.

As he looks at the Cross, with Christ suffering there, the Righteous One *for* the unrighteous, he sees in that atoning death the only sufficient foundation for his faith in God's pardoning mercy. In becoming our substitute, bearing our curse and dying in our place, Christ atones for our sin and so gives us peace. As a believer understands how Christ's righteousness becomes his very own, and how, in the strength of that, he is counted righteous before God, he feels that he has what he needs to restore him to God's favor: "Having been justified by faith, we have peace with God" (Romans 5:1). The new Christian seeks to wear this robe of righteousness by ever-renewed faith in the glorious gift of righteousness that has been given to him.

But as time goes on, and he seeks to grow in the Christian life, new needs arise. He wants to understand more fully how it is that God can justify the ungodly on the strength of the righteousness of another. He finds the answer in the wonderful teaching of Scripture about true union of the believer with Christ as the Second Adam (Romans 5:12–21). He sees that it is possible because Christ made himself one with His people, and they were one with Him. In perfect accordance with all law in the kingdom of nature and of heaven, each member of the body has full benefit from the deeds and the suffering experienced by the Head. And so he is led to understand that it is only as he fully realizes his personal union with Christ as the Head that he can truly experience the power of His righteousness, which brings his soul into full fellowship with the Holy One. The work of Christ does not become less precious with this understanding, but the person of Christ becomes more so; the work leads up into the very heart, the love and the life of the God-man.

And this experience sheds its light again upon Scripture. It leads him to notice what he had overlooked before: how distinctly the righteousness of God, as it becomes ours, is connected with the person of the Redeemer. "This is His name whereby He shall be called, the Lord our righteousness" (Jeremiah 23:6). "Surely in the Lord have I righteousness and strength" (Isaiah 45:24). "That we might become the righteousness of God in Him" (2 Corinthians 5:21). "That I may gain Christ and be found *in Him*, not having my own righteousness which is from the law, but that which is through faith in Christ, the righteousness which is from God by faith" (Philippians 3: 8–9). The believer finally sees how inseparable righteousness and life in Christ are from each other: ". . . by one Man's righteous act the free gift came to all men, resulting in *justification of life*" (Romans 5:18). "Those who receive abundance of grace and of the gift of righteousness will *reign in life* through the

One, Jesus Christ" (Romans 5:17). And he understands what deep meaning there is in the key word of Paul's letter to the Romans: "The righteous will *live* by faith" (Romans 1:17 NIV). Now he is not content with only thinking of his robe of imputed righteousness that was given to him through the Atonement. He sees beyond this to the possibility of putting on Jesus Christ, and being wrapped up in and clothed with *Jesus himself and His life*; he knows how completely the righteousness of God is his because the Lord our righteousness is his. Before he understood this, he felt too often that it was difficult to wear his white robe all day; it was as if he had to put it on deliberately when he came into God's presence to confess his sins and seek new grace. But now the living Christ himself is his righteousness—that Christ who watches over, keeps, and loves us as His own; so it is no longer an impossibility to walk all day in the robe of his loving presence.

Such an experience leads still further. Christ's life and righteousness are inseparably linked, and the believer becomes more conscious than before of a righteous nature planted within him. The new man created in Christ Jesus, is "created according to God, in righteousness and true holiness" (Ephesians 4:24). "He who practices righteousness is righteous, just as He is righteous" (1 John 3:7). The union to Jesus has changed not only our relationship to God but also our personal state before God. And as this intimate fellowship is maintained, the growing renewal of the whole being makes righteousness our very nature.

To a Christian who begins to see the deep meaning of the truth that He was made to us righteousness, it is hardly necessary to say, "Abide in Him." As long as he only thought of the righteousness of the substitute, and our being counted judicially righteous for His sake, the absolute necessity of *abiding in Him* was not apparent. But as the glory of "the Lord our righteousness" unfolds to the view, he sees that abiding in Him personally is the only way to stand, at all times, complete and accepted before God, because it is the only way to realize how the new and righteous nature can be strengthened from Jesus our Head. To the repentant sinner the chief thought was *the righteousness* that comes through Jesus' dying for sin; to the intelligent and growing believer, *Jesus,* the Living One, through whom the righteousness comes, is everything, because in having Him, he has His righteousness too.

Believer, abide in Christ as your righteousness. You still have within you a nature altogether corrupt, which is always trying to rise up and discourage your sense of acceptance and access to unbroken fellowship with the Father. Nothing can enable you to dwell and walk in the light of God, without even the shadow of a cloud between, but habitual abiding in Christ as your righteousness. To this you are called. Seek to walk worthy of that calling. Yield yourself to the Holy Spirit to reveal to you the wonderful grace that permits you to draw near to God, clothed in a divine righteousness. Take time to realize that the King's own robe has been put on you, and in it you need not fear entering His presence. It is the token that you are the man or woman the King delights to honor. Take time to remember that as much as you need this robe of righteousness in the palace, you require it even more when He sends you forth into the world, where you are the King's messenger and representative.

Live your daily life in full consciousness of being righteous in God's sight, an object of delight and pleasure in Christ.

Connect every view you have of Christ in His other graces with this first one: Christ Jesus—our righteousness from God. This will keep you in perfect peace. You will enter into, and dwell in, the rest of God. And your inmost being will be transformed into being righteous and doing righteousness. In your heart and life it will become obvious where you dwell; abiding in Jesus Christ, the Righteous One, you will share His position, His character, and His blessedness. It is said of Him: "You have loved righteousness and hated wickedness; therefore God, your God, has set you above your companions by anointing you with the oil of joy" (Hebrews 1:9 NIV). This joy and gladness will be your portion too as you abide in Him.

He Is Your Sanctification

Of Him (God) you are in Christ Jesus, who became for us
wisdom from God—and righteousness and
SANCTIFICATION and redemption.

1 Corinthians 1:30

"Paul ... to the church of God which is at Corinth, to those who are *sanctified* in Christ Jesus, called to be *saints*"—this is how the chapter opens in which we are taught that Christ is our sanctification, our holiness. In the Old Testament, believers were called the righteous; in the New Testament they are called saints, holy ones sanctified in Christ Jesus. Holy is higher than righteous. Holiness in reference to God relates to His inmost being; righteousness has to do with God's dealings with His creatures. In man, righteousness is but a stepping-stone to holiness. It is in holiness that man can approach the nature of God (Matthew 5:48; 1 Peter 1:16). In the Old Testament it was righteousness that was found, while holiness was only typified. In Jesus Christ, the Holy One, and in His people, His saints or holy ones, it is first realized.

As in Scripture, and in our text, so also in personal

experience: Righteousness comes before holiness. When the believer first finds Christ as his righteousness, he has such joy in being righteous that he hardly considers the idea of holiness. But as he grows, the desire for holiness makes itself felt, and he wants to know what provision his God has made for supplying that need. A superficial acquaintance with God's plan leads to the view that while justification is God's work, by faith in Christ, sanctification is our work, to be performed under the influence of the gratitude we feel for the deliverance we have experienced, and by the aid of the Holy Spirit. But the sincere Christian soon finds how little gratitude can supply the power. When he thinks that more prayer will bring it, he finds that, indispensable as prayer is, it is not enough. Often the believer struggles hopelessly for years, until he listens to the teaching of the Spirit, as He glorifies Christ again, and reveals Christ, our sanctification, to be appropriated by faith alone.

Christ is made sanctification to us by God. Holiness is the very nature of God, and *that alone is holy which God takes possession of and fills with himself.* God's answer to the question "How could sinful man become holy?" is "Christ, the Holy One of God." In Him, the One sanctified by the Father and sent into the world, God's holiness was revealed in the flesh, incarnated and brought within reach of man. Jesus declares, "For their sakes I sanctify Myself, that they also may be sanctified by the truth" (John 17:19). There is no other way for us to become holy but by becoming partakers of the holiness of Christ. And there is no other way of this taking place than by our personal spiritual union with Him, so that through His Holy Spirit His holy life flows into us. "Of Him you are in Christ Jesus, who was made to us sanctification." Abiding by faith in Christ our sanctification is the simple secret of a holy life. The measure of sanctification will depend on the measure of abiding in Him. As the soul learns to wholly abide in Christ, the promise is increasingly fulfilled: "May the God of peace Himself sanctify you completely" (1 Thessalonians 5:23).

To illustrate this relationship between the measure of the abiding and the measure of sanctification experienced, let us consider the grafting of a tree, that instructive symbol of our union to Jesus. The illustration is suggested by the Savior's words, "Make a tree good and its fruit will be good" (Matthew 12:33 NIV). Now I can graft a tree so that only a single branch bears good fruit, while many of the natural branches remain and bear their old fruit—a type of believer in whom a small part of the life is sanctified, but in whom, from ignorance or other reasons, the carnal life in many respects still has full reign.

I also can graft a tree so that every branch is cut off, and the whole tree becomes renewed to bear good fruit. Yet unless I watch over the tendency of the stems to give sprouts, they may again rise and grow strong, and, robbing the new graft of the strength it needs, make it weak. Such are Christians who, apparently powerfully converted, forsake all to follow Christ, and yet after a time, through carelessness, allow old habits to regain their power. As a result, their Christian life and fruit are weakened. But if I want a tree to be completely good, I take it when it is young, and, cutting the stem off right to the ground, I graft it just where it emerges from the soil. I watch over every bud that might arise from the old nature until the flow of sap from the old roots into the new stem is so complete that the old life has, as it were, been entirely conquered and covered by the new. Here I have a tree entirely renewed, an emblem of the

Christian who has learned by entire consecration to surrender everything for Christ, and in wholehearted faith to abide in Him.

If, in this last case, the old tree were a reasonable being that could cooperate with the gardener, what would the gardener say to it? Something like this, probably: "Now yield yourself entirely to this new nature I have given you; repress every tendency of the old nature to give buds or sprouts. Let all your sap and all your life-powers rise up into this graft taken from the beautiful tree over there, which I have put on you; in this way, you will bring forth much fruit that is sweet to the taste." And the reply of the tree to the gardener would be: "When you graft me, do not spare a single branch; let everything of the old self, even the smallest bud, be destroyed, that I may no longer live in my own, but in that other life that was cut off and brought and put upon me. That way I will be completely new and good."

Could you later ask the renewed tree, as it was bearing abundant fruit, what it could say of itself, its answer would be this: "In me, that is, in my roots, there dwells no good thing. I am always inclined toward evil; the sap I collect from the soil is corrupt in nature, and ready to show itself in bearing evil fruit. But just when the sap rises into the sunshine to ripen into fruit, the wise gardener covers me with a new life, through which my sap is purified, and all my powers are renewed to bear good fruit. All I have to do is abide in what I have received. He cares for the immediate repression and removal of every bud which the old nature would still like to put forth."

Christian, do not be afraid to claim God's promises to make you holy. Don't listen to the suggestion that the corruption of your old nature renders holiness an impossibility. In your flesh dwells no good thing, that is true, and that flesh, though crucified with Christ, is not yet dead, but it continually seeks to rise up and lead you to evil. But the Father is your Vinedresser. He has grafted the life of Christ onto your life. That holy life is stronger than your evil life; under the watchful care of the Vinedresser, that new life can keep down the workings of the evil life within you. The evil nature is there, with its unchanged tendency to rise up and show itself. But the new nature is there too; the living Christ, your sanctification, is there, and through Him all your powers can be sanctified as they rise into life. And you will be able to bear fruit to the glory of the Father.

Now, if you would live a holy life, abide in Christ your sanctification. Look upon Him as the Holy One of God, made man that He might communicate to us the holiness of God. Listen when Scripture teaches that there is within you a new nature, a new man, created in Christ Jesus in righteousness *and true holiness.* Remember that this holy nature that is in you is especially made for living a holy life and performing all holy duties, as much as the old nature is suited for doing evil. Understand that this holy nature within you has its root and life in Christ in heaven, and can only grow and become strong as the interaction between it and its source is uninterrupted.

Above all, believe most confidently that Jesus Christ himself delights in maintaining that new nature within you, and giving to it His own strength and wisdom for its work. Let faith in this reality lead you daily to surrender all self-confidence, and confess the utter corruption of all there is in you by nature. Let it fill you with a quiet and assured confidence that you are well able to do what the Father expects of you as His child, under the covenant of His grace, because you have Christ strengthening you. Let it teach you to lay yourself and your services on the altar as spiritual sacrifices, holy and acceptable in His sight, a sweet-smelling fragrance. Do not look upon a life of holiness as a strain and an effort, but as the natural outgrowth of the life of Christ within you. Let a quiet, hopeful, gladsome faith assure you that all you need for a holy life will be given you out of the holiness of Jesus. Then you will understand and prove what it is to abide in Christ our sanctification.

He Is Your Redemption

*Of Him (God) you are in Christ Jesus, who became for us
wisdom from God—and righteousness and
sanctification and REDEMPTION.*

1 Corinthians 1:30

Here we reach the top of the ladder as it ascends into heaven—
the blessed end to which Christ and life in Him is to lead. The
word *redemption*, though sometimes applied to our deliverance
from the guilt of sin, here refers to our complete and final
deliverance from all the consequences of sin, when the
Redeemer's work will be fully displayed, even to the redemption
of the body itself (Romans 8:21–23; Ephesians 1:14; 4:30). The
expression points us to the highest glory to be hoped for in the
future, and therefore also to the highest blessing to be enjoyed
in the present in Christ. We have seen how, as a Prophet, Christ
is our wisdom, revealing to us God and His love, along with the
nature and conditions of the salvation that love has prepared.
As a Priest, He is our righteousness, restoring us to right relationship to God and securing for us His favor and friendship.
As a King, He is our sanctification, forming and guiding us into

obedience to the Father's holy will. As these three offices work out God's one purpose, the grand consummation will be reached: complete deliverance from sin and all its effects, and ransomed humanity regaining all that was lost in the Fall.

Christ is made *redemption* to us by God. The word invites us to look upon Jesus, not only as He lived on earth—teaching us by word and by example as He died to reconcile us with God, as He lives again, a victorious King, rising to receive His crown—but also as, sitting at the right hand of God, He takes again the glory which He had with the Father before the world began and holds it there for us. There His human nature, His human body, free from all the consequences of sin to which He once was exposed, is now in heaven sharing the divine glory. As Son of Man, He dwells on the throne and in the presence of the Father; the deliverance from what He had to suffer for sin is complete and eternal. Complete redemption is fulfilled and revealed in His own Person; what He as man is and has in heaven is the complete redemption. He is made of God to us redemption.

We are in Him as such. And to the extent that we can receive this truth as we abide in Him as our redemption, the more we will experience, even here, "the powers of the coming age" (Hebrews 6:5 NIV). As our communion with Him becomes more intimate and intense and we let the Holy Spirit reveal Him to us in His heavenly glory, the more we realize how the life in us is the life of One who sits upon the throne of heaven. We feel the power of an endless life working in us. We taste eternal life; we have a foretaste of the eternal glory.

The blessings flowing from abiding in Christ as our redemption are great. The soul is delivered from all fear of death. There was a time when even the Savior feared death. But no longer. He has triumphed over death; even His body has entered into God's glory. The believer who abides in Christ as his full redemption realizes even now his spiritual victory over death. It becomes to him the servant that removes the last rags of the old carnal robe before he is clothed with the new body of glory. Death carries the body to the grave, to lie there as the seed from which the new body will arise as a worthy companion of the glorified spirit. The resurrection of the body is no longer an empty doctrine, but a living expectation, because the Spirit of Him who raised Jesus from the dead dwells in the body as the pledge that even our mortal bodies will be made alive (Romans 8:11–23). Faith in this expectation exercises its sanctifying influence by making us willing to surrender the sinful members of our bodies to Him—to be put to death and then subjected to the reign of the Spirit, as preparation for the time when our frail bodies will be changed to be fashioned like His glorious body (Philippians 3:21).

This full redemption of Christ as extending to the body has a depth of meaning not easily expressed. It was of man as a whole, soul and body, that it was said that he was made in the image and likeness of God. In the angels, God created spirits without material bodies; in the creation of the world, there was matter without spirit. Man was to be the highest specimen of divine art: the combination in one being of matter and spirit in perfect harmony, as a type of the most perfect union between God and His own creation. Sin entered in and appeared to block the divine plan. By sin the material obtained a dreaded supremacy over the spiritual. But God's plan was still in place.

The Word was *made flesh*, the divine fullness received an

embodiment in the humanity of Christ so that redemption might be complete and perfect; the whole creation, which now groans and labors in pain together, will be delivered from the bondage of corruption into the liberty of the glory of the children of God (Romans 8:21–22). God's purpose will not be accomplished, and Christ's glory will not be fully exhibited, until the body, which includes the whole of nature, has been transformed by the power of the spiritual life. It will then become the transparent garment that will shine forth with radiance as it reflects the glory of the Infinite Spirit. Only then will we understand the depth of meaning in these words: "Christ Jesus was made to us (complete) redemption."

In the meantime we know that: "Of Him (God) you are in Christ Jesus," as your redemption. This is not meant to be merely a future revelation; we must seek to enter into and apply it in our present abiding in Christ so that we may reach full development in the Christian life. We do this as we learn to triumph over our fear of death. We learn to look upon Christ as the Lord of our body, claiming its entire consecration on this side of heaven and victory over the terrible dominion sin has enjoyed in the body. Another way we do this is learning to look on all nature as part of the kingdom of Christ, destined, even though it might be through a baptism of fire, to take part in His redemption. We do it as we allow the powers of the coming age to possess us and to lift us up into a life in the heavenly places, to enlarge our hearts and our views, to anticipate, even here, the things which have never entered into the heart of man to imagine (1 Corinthians 2:9).

Believer, abide in Christ as your redemption. Let this be the crown of your Christian life. It is faithfulness in the previous steps of your Christian life that will best fit you for this spiritual reality. Abide in Him as your wisdom, the perfect revelation of all that God is and has for you. Follow, in the daily ordering of your inner and outer life, His teaching with humility, and you will be counted worthy to have secrets revealed to you, secrets that to most disciples are a sealed book. Such wisdom will lead you into the mysteries of our complete redemption.

Abide in Him as your righteousness, and dwell clothed with Him in that inner sanctuary of the Father's favor and presence to which His righteousness gives you access. As you rejoice in your reconciliation, you will understand how it includes all things, even full redemption; "For it pleased the Father that in Him all fullness should dwell, and by Him to reconcile all things to Himself, by Him, whether things on earth or things in heaven" (Colossians 1:19–20). And abide in Him as your sanctification; the experience of His power to make you holy in spirit, soul, and body will make your faith alive in a holiness that will not stop working until the bells of the horses and every pot in Jerusalem shall be holiness to the Lord (Zechariah 14:20–21).

Abide in Him as your redemption, and live, even here, as the heir of future glory. As you seek to experience on earth the full power of His saving grace, your heart will be enlarged to realize the position mankind has been destined to occupy in the universe, with all things made subject to Him. For your part, you can be assured that you will be readied by the Spirit of God to live worthy of that high and heavenly calling.

The Crucified One

*I have been crucified with Christ: it is no longer I who live,
but Christ lives in me.*

Galatians 2:20

We have been united together in the likeness of His death.

Romans 6:5

"I have been crucified with Christ": Here the apostle expresses his assurance of his fellowship with Christ in His sufferings and death, and his full participation in all the power and the blessing of that death. The apostle Paul was so convinced of this and the fact that he was now indeed dead that he adds: "It is *no longer I who live*, but Christ lives in me." How blessed must be the experience of such a union with the Lord Jesus—to be able to look upon His death as mine, just as really as it was His, to look upon His perfect obedience to God, His victory over sin, and complete deliverance from its power as mine, and to realize that the power of that death works by faith daily with a divine energy to put to death the flesh, to renew the whole life into perfect conformity to the resurrection life of Jesus! Abiding in

Jesus, the Crucified One, is the secret to the growth of that new life, which comes from the death of our old life.

Let us try to understand this. The suggestive expression "*united together* in the likeness of His death," will teach us what abiding in the Crucified One means. When a graft is united with the stock on which it is to grow, we know that it must be kept fixed; it must abide in the place where the stock has been cut and wounded to make an opening to receive the graft. No graft is possible without wounding, laying bare and opening up the inner life of the tree to receive the foreign branch. It is only through such wounding that access can be obtained to the fellowship of the sap and the growth and life of the stronger stem.

This reality holds true for the relationship between Jesus and the sinner. Only when we are united together in the likeness of His death will we also be in the likeness of His resurrection, partakers of the life and the power that are in Him. In the death of the Cross Christ was wounded, and in His opened wounds a place was prepared where we might be grafted in. And just as one might say to a graft as it is fixed in its place, "Abide here in the wound of the stem, it will now bear you"; so to the believing soul the message comes, "Abide in the wounds of Jesus; there is the place of union, life, and growth. There you will see how His heart was opened to receive you; His flesh was torn so that the way might be opened for your being made one with Him, and having access to all the blessings flowing from His divine nature."

You have also noticed how the graft has to be torn away from the tree where it naturally grew and cut into conformity to the place prepared for it in the wounded stem. Even so the believer has to be made conformable to Christ's death—to be crucified and to die with Him. The wounded stem and the wounded graft are cut to fit into each other, into each other's likeness. There is a fellowship between Christ's sufferings and your sufferings. His experiences must become yours. The disposition He showed in choosing and bearing the Cross must be yours. Like Him, you will have to give full assent to the righteous judgment and curse of a holy God against sin. Like Him, you have to consent to yield your life, the old nature full of sin and its curse, to death, and through it to pass to the new life. Like Him, you will experience that it is only through the self-sacrifice of Gethsemane and Calvary that the path to the joy and fruit-bearing of the resurrection life can be found. The more clear the resemblance between the wounded stem and the wounded graft, the more exactly their wounds fit into each other, and the more complete will be the union and the growth.

It is in Jesus, the Crucified One, I must abide. I must learn to look upon the Cross as not only atonement to God but also a victory over the devil; it is not only deliverance from the guilt but also from the power of sin. I must gaze on Him on the Cross, seeing Him as the One who offered himself in order to receive me into the closest possible union and fellowship. Through Him I can partake of the full power of His death to sin and the new life of victory to which it is but the gateway. My part is simply to yield myself to Him in undivided surrender, with much prayer and strong desire, asking to be admitted into the ever-closer fellowship and conformity of His death by the power of the Spirit in which He died that death.

Let me try to understand why the Cross is thus the place of union. *On the Cross* the Son of God enters into the greatest union with man—enters into the experience of what it means to become a son of man, a member of a race under the curse. It is in death that the Prince of life conquers the power of death; it is in death alone that He can enable me to partake of that victory. The life He imparts is a life from the dead; each new experience of the power of that life depends upon the fellowship of the death. The death and the life are inseparable. All of the grace that Jesus the Saving One gives is given only in the path of fellowship with Jesus the Crucified One.

Christ came and took my place; I must put myself in His place, and abide there. And there is but one place that is both His and mine—that place is the Cross: His place because of His free choice; my place because of the curse of sin. He came there to seek me; there alone can I find Him. When He found me there, it was the place of cursing; this He experienced, for "Cursed is everyone who hangs on a tree" (Galatians 3:13). But He made it a place of blessing; this I experienced because Christ delivered us from the curse, being made a curse for us. When Christ comes in my place, He remains what He was, the beloved of the Father; but in fellowship with me He shares my curse and dies my death.

When I stand in His place, which is still always mine, I am still what I was by nature, the cursed one, who deserves to die; but since I am united to Him, I share His blessing and receive His life. When He came to be one with me He could not avoid the Cross, for the curse always points to the Cross as its end and fruit. And when I seek to be one with Him, I cannot avoid the Cross, either; for life and deliverance are to be found only in the Cross. As inevitably as my curse pointed Him to the Cross as the only place where He could be fully united to me, His blessing points me to the Cross too as the only place where

I can be united to Him. He took my cross for His own; I must take His Cross as my own; I must be crucified with Him. It is as I abide daily, deeply in Jesus the Crucified One that I will taste the sweetness of His love, the power of His life, and the completeness of His salvation.

It is a deep mystery, this Cross of Christ. I am afraid there are many Christians who are content to look upon the Cross, with Christ on it dying for their sins, who have little heart for fellowship with the Crucified One. They hardly know that He invites them to it. Or they are content to consider the ordinary afflictions of life, of which the world's children often have as many as they do, as their share of Christ's Cross. They have no understanding of what it means to be crucified with Christ, not knowing that bearing the Cross means likeness to Christ in the principles that propelled Him in His path of obedience. The entire surrender of all self-will, the complete denial to the flesh of its every desire and pleasure, the perfect separation from the world in all its ways of thinking and acting, the losing and hating of one's life, the giving up of self and its interests for the sake of others—this is the disposition that marks him who has taken up Christ's Cross, who seeks to say, "I am crucified with Christ; I abide in Christ, the Crucified One."

Would you please your Lord and live in as close fellowship with Him as His grace could maintain in you? Then pray that His Spirit will lead you into this blessed truth, this secret of the Lord for those who fear Him. We know how Peter knew and confessed Christ as the Son of the living God while the Cross was still an offense to him (Matthew 16:16–17, 21, 23). The faith that believes in the blood that pardons, and the life that renews, can only reach its perfect growth as it abides beneath the Cross and in living fellowship with Him seeks for perfect conformity with Jesus the Crucified.

Jesus, our crucified Redeemer, teach us not only to believe on you but also to abide in you. Help us to take your Cross not only as the ground of our pardon but also as the law of our life. May we learn to love it not only because on it you bore our curse but also because on it we enter into intimate fellowship with you and are crucified with you. As we yield ourselves fully to be filled with the Spirit in which you bore the Cross, teach us how to be made partakers of the power and the blessing found only in the Cross.

God Himself Will Establish You in Him

*He who establishes us with you in Christ and
has anointed us is God.*

2 Corinthians 1:21

These words of Paul teach us a much-needed and most blessed truth—that just as our first being united with Christ was the work of divine omnipotence, so we may also look to the Father for being kept and being established more firmly in Him. "The Lord will perfect that which concerns me" (Psalm 138:8)—this expression of confidence should always accompany the prayer "Do not forsake the works of Your hands" (Psalm 138:8). In all his longings and prayers to reach a deeper and more perfect abiding in Christ, the believer must have this confidence: "He who began a good work in you will carry it on to completion until the day of Christ Jesus" (Philippians 1:6 NIV). There is nothing that will so help to root and ground him in Christ as faith in these words: "He who establishes us in Christ is God."

How many there are who can witness to the fact that this

faith is just what they need! They continually mourn over the ups and downs of their spiritual life. Sometimes there are hours and days of great continuity and even a profound experience of the grace of God. But how little is needed to mar their peace, to bring a cloud over the soul! And then, how the faith is shaken. All efforts to regain their standing appear utterly fruitless; and neither solemn vows, nor watching and prayer, help to restore to them the peace they had for a while tasted. What they need to understand is how their own efforts are the cause of their failure, because it is God alone who can establish us in Christ Jesus.

Just as in justification they had to cease from their own working, and to accept in faith the promise that God would give them life in Christ, so now, in the matter of their sanctification, their first need is *to cease from striving themselves to establish the connection with Christ more firmly, and to allow God to do it.* "God is faithful, by whom you were called into the fellowship of His Son, Jesus Christ our Lord" (1 Corinthians 1:9). What they need is simple faith in the fact that establishing us in Christ, day by day, is God's work—a work that He delights to do, in spite of all our weakness and unfaithfulness, if we will but trust Him for it.

Many can testify to the blessedness of such a faith and the experience it brings. What peace and rest to know that there is a Vinedresser who cares for the branch, to see that it grows stronger, and that its union with the Vine becomes more perfect, who watches over every hindrance and danger and supplies every need! What peace and rest to fully and finally give up our abiding into the care of God, and to never have a wish or thought, never offer a prayer or engage in an exercise connected with it, without first gladly remembering that what we do is only the manifestation of what God is doing in us! The establishing in Christ is His work: He accomplishes it by stirring us to watch, wait, and work. But this He can do with power only as we stop interrupting Him by our self-working, as we accept in faith the dependent posture that honors Him and opens the heart to let Him work. How such a faith frees the soul from care and responsibility! In the midst of the rush and bustle of the world's busy life, the subtle and ceaseless temptations to sin, and all the daily cares and trials that so easily distract and lead to failure, how wonderful to be an established Christian who is always abiding in Christ! How blessed even to have the faith that such a position can be attained and is within our reach!

Dear believer, the blessing is indeed within your reach. He who establishes you with us in Christ *is God.* What I want you to take in is this: Believing this promise will not only give you comfort but will also be the means of obtaining your desire. You know how Scripture teaches us that in all God's leadings with His people faith has everywhere been the one condition for seeing His power manifested. Faith is the ceasing from all our natural efforts and all other dependence; faith is confessed helplessness casting itself upon God's promise and claiming its fulfillment; faith is putting ourselves quietly into God's hands for Him to do His work. What you and I need now is to take time, until this truth stands out before us in all its spiritual brightness: It is God Almighty, God the Faithful and Gracious One, who has undertaken to establish me in Christ Jesus.

Listen to what the Word teaches you: "The Lord *will establish* you as a holy people to Himself" (Deuteronomy 28:9); "Your

God has loved Israel, to *establish* them forever" (2 Chronicles 9:8); "Now to Him who is able *to establish you*, be glory through Jesus Christ forever" (Romans 16:25, 27); "So that He *may establish your hearts blameless in holiness*" (1 Thessalonians 3:13); "The Lord is faithful, who will establish you and guard you from the evil one" (2 Thessalonians 3:3); "The God of all grace, who has called us to His eternal glory by Christ Jesus, after you have suffered a while, perfect, *establish*, strengthen, and settle you" (1 Peter 5:10). Can you take these words to mean anything less than that you too—however spasmodic your spiritual life has been up to now, however unfavorable your natural character or your circumstances may appear—can be established in Christ Jesus? If we take the time to listen, in simple childlike humility, to these words as the truth of God, the confidence will come: As surely as I am in Christ, I will also, day by day, be established in Him.

The lesson appears so simple; and yet most of us take so long to learn it. The main reason is that the grace the promise offers is so large, so Godlike, so beyond all our thoughts, that we do not take it to mean what it says. The believer who has finally come to see and accept what it brings can testify to the wonderful change that comes over the spiritual life. Before he had taken control of his own welfare; now he has God to take charge of it. He now knows himself to be in the school of God, with a Teacher who plans the whole course of study for each of His pupils with infinite wisdom, and delights to have them come daily for the lessons He has to give. All he asks is to feel himself constantly in God's hands and to follow His guidance, neither lagging behind nor getting ahead of Him. Remembering that it is God who works both to will and to do, he sees his only safety in yielding himself to God's working. He lays aside all anxiety about his inner life and its growth, because the Father is the Vinedresser. Under His wise and watchful care each plant is well secured. He knows that there is the prospect of a most blessed life of strength and fruitfulness to every one who will take God wholly as his only hope.

Believer, you must admit that such a life of trust is most blessed. You say, perhaps, that there are times when you do, with your whole heart, consent to this way of living and wholly abandon the care of your inner life to your Father. But somehow it does not last. You forget again; and instead of beginning each morning with the joyous transference of all the needs and cares of your spiritual life to the Father's charge, you again feel anxious, burdened, and helpless.

Could it be that you have not committed to the Father's care this matter, daily remembering to renew your entire surrender? Memory is one of the highest powers in our nature. By it day is linked to day, the unity of life through all our years is kept up, and we know that we are still ourselves. In the spiritual life, recollection is of infinite value. For the sanctifying of our memory, in the service of our spiritual life, God has provided most beautifully. The Holy Spirit is the Spirit of recollection. Jesus said, "He will bring to your remembrance all things that I said to you" (John 14:26). "He who *establishes* us with you in Christ is God, who also has *sealed* us and *given us the Spirit in our hearts* as a deposit" (2 Corinthians 1:21–22). It is for the purpose of establishing us that the Holy Spirit has been given. God's blessed promises, and your unceasing acts of faith and surrender that accept them—He will enable you to remember these each day. The Holy Spirit is—praise be to God—the memory of the new man.

Apply this to the promise of the text: "He who establishes us in Christ is God." As you now, at this moment, abandon all anxiety about your growth and progress to the God who has undertaken to establish you in the Vine, and feel what a joy it is to know that God alone has charge, ask and trust Him by the Holy Spirit to always remind you of your blessed relationship with Him. He will do it; and with each new morning your faith may grow stronger and brighter: The Father will see that each day I become more firmly united to Christ.

And now, beloved fellow-believer, "the God of all grace, who called us to His eternal glory by Christ Jesus, *perfect, establish, strengthen, and settle you*" (1 Peter 5:10). What more can you desire? Expect it confidently, ask for it fervently. Count on God to do His work. And learn in faith to sing the song, the notes of which each new experience will make deeper and sweeter: "Now to Him who is able to *establish* you, be glory through Jesus Christ forever. Amen" (Romans 16:25, 27). Yes, glory to God, who has undertaken to establish us in Christ!

Every Moment

*In that day sing to her, "A vineyard of red wine! I, the Lord,
keep it, I water it every moment; Lest any hurt it,
I keep it night and day."*

Isaiah 27:2–3

The vineyard was the symbol of the people of Israel, in whose midst the True Vine was to stand. The branch is the symbol of the individual believer, who stands in the Vine. The song of the vineyard is also the song of the Vine and its every branch. The command still goes out to the watchers of the vineyard—if only they would obey it, and sing till every fainthearted believer learned and joined the joyful strain—"Sing to her: I, the Lord, *keep it;* I water it *every moment;* Lest any hurt it, I *keep* it night and day."

What an answer from the mouth of God himself to the question so often asked: Is it possible for the believer to always abide in Jesus? Is a life of unbroken fellowship with the Son of God possible here in this earthly life? If abiding is our work, to be done in our strength, then the answer must be no. But thankfully the things that are impossible with men are possible with God. If the Lord himself will keep the soul night and day, and watch it and water it every moment, then surely uninterrupted communion with Jesus does become a blessed possibility to those who can trust God to mean and to do what He says.

In one sense, it is true, all believers are always abiding in Jesus; without this there could not be true spiritual life. "If anyone does not abide in Me, he is cast out" (John 15:6). But when the Savior gives the command "Abide in Me" with the promise "He who abides in Me bears much fruit" (John 15:4–5), He speaks of that willing, intelligent, and wholehearted surrender by which we accept His offer and consent to abiding in Him as the only life we choose or seek. The objections that are raised against our right to expect that we will be able to, voluntarily and consciously, abide always in Jesus are mainly two.

One is derived from the nature of man. It is said that our limited powers prevent us from being occupied with two things at the same moment. God's providence places many Christians in business, where for hours at a time close attention to the work they have to do is required. How can such a man, it is asked, with his whole mind on the work he has to do, be at the same time occupied with Christ and keep up fellowship with Him? The consciousness of abiding in Jesus is seen as requiring such a strain, and such a direct occupation of the mind with heavenly thoughts, that to enjoy the blessing would imply a withdrawing of oneself from all the ordinary activities of life. This is the same error that drove the first monks into the wilderness.

Praise be to God, there is no necessity for such a going out of the world. Abiding in Jesus is not a work that needs our minds to be engaged each moment, or our attention to be directly and actively occupied with it. It is an entrusting of ourselves to the keeping of Eternal Love, in the faith that it will abide near us and with its holy presence watch over us and ward off evil, even when we have to be intently occupied with other things. In this way the heart has rest, peace, and joy in the consciousness of being kept when it cannot keep itself.

In ordinary life, we have many illustrations of the influence of a supreme love reigning in and guarding the soul while the mind concentrates itself on work that requires its whole attention. Think of the father of a family, separated for a time from his home so that he may secure for his loved ones what they need. He loves his wife and children and longs to return to them. There may be hours of intense occupation when he does not have a moment to think of them, and yet his love is as deep and real as when he can recall their images. All the while his love and the hope of making them happy urge him on and fill him with a secret joy in his work. Think of a king: In the midst of work, pleasure, and trial, he all the while acts under the secret influence of the consciousness of royalty, even while he is unaware of it. A loving wife and mother never for one moment loses the sense of her relationship to her husband and children; the consciousness and the love are there, even among all her engagements.

In the same way, it is not impossible to see how everlasting love can so take and keep possession of our spirits that we too will never for a moment lose the secret consciousness: We are in Christ, kept in Him by His almighty power. Oh, it is possible; we can be sure it is. Our abiding in Jesus is even more than a fellowship of love—it is a fellowship of life. In work or in rest, the consciousness of life never leaves us. And even so can the mighty power of Eternal Life maintain within us the consciousness of its presence. Or rather, Christ, who is our life, himself dwells within us, and by His presence maintains our consciousness that we are in Him.

The second objection has reference to our sinfulness. Christians are so accustomed to looking upon sinning daily as something absolutely inevitable, they regard it as indisputable that no one can keep up abiding fellowship with the Savior; we must sometimes be unfaithful and fail. But it is precisely because we have a sinful nature that abiding in Christ has been ordained for us as our sufficient—and only—deliverance! After all, it is the Heavenly Vine, the living, loving Christ, in whom we have to abide; and His almighty power to hold us fast should be the measure of our expectations! We cannot imagine our Lord giving us the command "Abide in Me" without securing the grace and the power to enable us to perform it! We must remember that we have the Father as the Vinedresser to keep us from falling, and not in a large and general sense, but according to His own precious promise: "Night and day, every moment" (Isaiah 27:2–3). If we will only look to our God as our Keeper we will learn to believe that conscious abiding in Christ every moment, night and day, is indeed what God has prepared for them who love Him.

My beloved fellow Christians, let nothing less than this be your aim. I know that you may not find it easy to attain; there may come more than one hour of weary struggle and bitter failure. Were the church of Christ what it should be—were older believers to younger converts what they should be, witnesses to God's faithfulness, like Caleb and Joshua, encouraging their brethren to go up and possess the land with their good report, "If the Lord delights in us, then He will bring us into this land" (Numbers 14:8), and were the atmosphere which the young believer breathes as he enters the fellowship of the saints that of a healthy, trusting, joyful consecration—abiding in Christ would come as the natural outgrowth of being in Him. But such a great part of the body is in what can only be described as a sickly state that believers who are pressing after this blessing are hindered by the depressing influence of both the thought and the life of others in the body. It is not to discourage that I say this, but to warn, and to urge us to cast ourselves entirely upon the Word of God himself. You may have moments when you are ready to give in to despair. But be of good courage; only believe. He who has put the blessing within your reach will assuredly lead to its possession.

The way in which we receive this blessing may differ. To some it may come as the gift of a moment. In times of revival, in fellowship with other believers in whom the Spirit is working effectually, under the leading of some servant of God who can guide, and sometimes in solitude too it is as if all at once a new revelation comes upon the soul. It sees, as in the light of heaven, the strong Vine holding and bearing the weak branches so securely that doubt becomes impossible. When this happens. we wonder how we could ever have understood the words to mean anything else but this: To abide unceasingly in Christ is the portion of every believer. When the soul sees it and believes it, rejoicing and love will come as the inevitable response.

To others it comes by a slower and more difficult path. Day by day, amid discouragement and difficulty, the soul has to press forward. If this is your situation, hear the Savior say, "Be of good cheer" (John 16:33); this way, too, leads to the rest. Only seek to keep your heart set upon the promise "I the Lord keep it, night and day." Take from His own lips the watchword *"Every moment."* In that, you have the law of His love and the law of your hope. Be content with nothing less. Do not allow your mind to think that the duties and cares, the sorrows and sins of this life, must succeed in hindering the abiding life of fellowship. Take rather the language of faith for the rule of your daily experience: I am persuaded that neither death with its fears, nor life with its cares, nor things present with their pressing claims, nor things to come with their dark shadows, nor height of joy, nor depth of sorrow, nor any other creature, shall be able, for one single moment, to separate us from the love of God which is in Christ Jesus our Lord (see Romans 8:38–39). And it is this love in which He is teaching me to abide. If things look dark and faith would fail, sing again the song of the vineyard: "I the Lord keep it, I water it every moment; Lest any hurt it, I keep it night and day." And be assured that if God the Father keeps the branch night and day, and waters it every moment, a life of continuous and unbroken fellowship with Christ is indeed our privilege.

Day by Day

The people are to go out each day and gather enough for that day.

Exodus 16:4 (NIV)

Enough for that day: Such was the rule for God's giving and man's working in the gathering of the manna. It is still the law in all the dealings of God's grace with His children. A clear insight into the beauty and application of this arrangement is a wonderful help in understanding how one, who feels himself utterly weak, can have the confidence and the perseverance to hold on brightly through all his earthly years. A patient who had been in a serious accident once asked a doctor: "Doctor, how long will I have to lie here?" The answer, "Only a day at a time," taught the patient a precious lesson. It was the same lesson God recorded for His people of all ages long before: enough for that day.

It was, without doubt, with a view to this and to meet man's weakness that God graciously appointed the change of day and night. If time had been given to man in the form of one long, unbroken day, it would have exhausted and overwhelmed him;

the change of day and night continually replenishes his strength. Children are given only one lesson for the day and in that way master the entire book in time. It would be useless to give the whole book to them at once; so it is with grown men too. Because divisions of time are broken down and divided into small fragments, we can bear them; only the care and the work of each day have to be undertaken—enough for that day only. The rest of the night enables us to make a fresh start with each new morning; the mistakes of the past can be avoided, its lessons improved. And we have only each day to be faithful for the one short day, and long years and a long life take care of themselves without the sense of their length or their weight ever being a burden.

Most sweet is the encouragement to be derived from this truth in the life of grace. Many a soul is upset with the thought as to how it will be able to gather and to keep the manna needed for all its years of travel through such a barren wilderness. It has not learned what unspeakable comfort there is in the word *enough for that day*. That word completely takes away all care for tomorrow. Only today is yours; tomorrow is the Father's. The question "What security do you have that during all the years in which you have to battle the coldness, temptations, or trials of the world, you will always abide in Jesus?" is one you need not, may not ask. Manna, as your food and strength, is given only by the day; to faithfully fill the present is your only security for the future. Accept, enjoy, and fulfill with your whole heart the part you have to perform this day. His presence and grace enjoyed today will remove all doubt as to whether you can entrust tomorrow to Him too.

What great value this truth teaches us to attach to each

single day! We are so easily led to look at life as a great big whole, and to neglect the little today, to forget that the single days do indeed make up the whole, and that the value of each single day depends on its influence on the whole. One day lost is a link broken in the chain, which it often takes more than another day to mend. One day lost influences the next and makes its keeping more difficult. In fact, one day lost may be the loss of what months or years of careful labor had secured. The experience of many a believer would confirm this.

Believer, would you abide in Jesus? Let it be day by day. You have already heard the message of "Moment by Moment"; the lesson of "Day by Day" has even more to teach. Of the moments there are many where there is no direct exercise of the mind on your part; the abiding is in the deeper recesses of the heart, kept by the Father, to whom you entrusted yourself. But this is precisely the work that with each new day has to be renewed for the day—the distinct renewal of surrender and trust for the life of moment by moment. God has gathered up the moments and bound them up into a bundle (1 Samuel 25:29) for the very purpose that we might measure them. As we look forward in the morning, or look back in the evening, and weigh the moments, we learn how to value and how to use them rightly.

As the Father, with each new morning, meets you with the promise of sufficient manna for the day for yourself and those who have to partake with you, meet Him with the bright and loving renewal of your acceptance of the position He has given you in His beloved Son. Accustom yourself to look upon this as one of the reasons for the appointment of day and night. God thought of our weakness and sought to provide for it. Let each day derive its value from your calling to abide in Christ. As its light opens on your waking eyes, accept it on these terms: a day, just one day only, but still a day, given to abide and grow up in Jesus Christ. Whether it be a day of health or sickness, joy or sorrow, rest or work, of struggle or victory, let the main thought with which you receive it in the morning thanksgiving be this: "A day that the Father gave; in it I may, I must become more closely united to Jesus." As the Father asks, "Can you trust Me for just this one day to keep you abiding in Jesus, and Jesus to keep you fruitful?" you are compelled to give the joyful response: "I will trust and not be afraid."

The day's portion, enough for the day, was given to Israel in the morning very early. The portion was for use and nourishment during the whole day, but the giving and the getting of it was the morning's work. This suggests how greatly the power to abide all the day in Jesus depends on the morning hour. "If the firstfruit is holy, the batch is also holy" (Romans 11:16). Hours of intense occupation come during the day in the rush of business or the pressure of deadlines, when only the Father's keeping can ensure the connection with Jesus remains unbroken.

The morning manna fed the Israelites all day; it is only when the believer in the morning secures his quiet time in secret to effectively renew loving fellowship with his Savior that abiding in Christ can be kept up all day. But what cause for thanksgiving that it can be done! In the morning, with its freshness and quiet, the believer can look out upon the day. He can consider its duties and its temptations, and go over them beforehand, as it were, with his Savior, casting all upon Him who has promised to be everything to him. Christ is his manna, his nourishment, his strength, and his life; he can take enough for that day, Christ being his for all the needs the day may bring. In this way the believer can proceed with the assurance that his day will be one of blessing and growth.

And then, as the lesson of the value and the work of the single day is being taken to heart, the learner is unconsciously being led on to perceive the secret of "day by day continually" (Exodus 29:38). The blessed abiding grasped by faith for each day apart is an unceasing and ever-increasing growth. Each day of faithfulness brings a blessing for the next, making both the trust and the surrender easier and more blessed. And so the Christian life grows; as we give our whole heart to the work of each day. And so each day separately, all the day continually, and day by day successively, we abide in Jesus.

The days make up the life; what once appeared too high and too great to attain is given to the soul that was content to take and use "enough for the day, as prescribed for each day" (Ezra 3:4 NIV). Even here on earth the voice is heard: "Well done, good and faithful servant; you have been faithful over a few things, I will make you ruler over many things. Enter into the joy of your master" (Matthew 25:23). Our daily life becomes a wonderful interchange of God's daily grace and our daily praise: "Who daily loads us with His benefits" (Psalm 68:19); "that I may daily perform my vows" (Psalm 61:8). God's reason for daily giving is understood as we see how He gives only enough but also fully enough for each day.

We are encouraged to adopt His way, the way of daily asking and expecting. We begin to number our days not from the sun's rising over the world, or by the work we do or the food we eat, but by the daily renewal of the miracle of the manna—the blessing of daily fellowship with Him who is the Life and the Light of the world. The heavenly life is as unbroken and continuous as the earthly; abiding in Christ each day brings to that day sufficient blessing. And so we learn to abide in Him every day, all through the day.

Lord, help us to see that this is enough—for today and every day to come.

At This Moment

Behold, now is the accepted time; behold,
now is the day of salvation.

2 Corinthians 6:2

Looking at abiding in Christ from our perspective, the thought of living moment to moment is of such central importance that we should speak of it once more. And to all who desire to learn the blessed art of living only a moment at a time, we want to say: The way to learn it is to exercise yourself in living in the present moment. Each time your attention is free to occupy itself with the thought of Jesus—whether it be with time to think and pray, or only for a few passing seconds—let your first thought be to say: "Now, at this moment, I do abide in Jesus." Do not use such time in vain regrets that you have not been abiding fully, or in still more hurtful fears that you will not be able to abide, but rather take the position the Father has given you: "I am in Christ; this is the place God has given me. I accept it; here I rest; I do now abide in Jesus." This is the way to learn to abide continually.

You may be yet so weak as to fear to say of each day, "I am

abiding in Jesus"; but the weakest believer can, each single moment, say, as he agrees to occupy his place as a branch in the Vine, "Yes, I do abide in Christ." It is not a matter of feeling, or a question of growth or strength in the Christian life; rather, it is simply a question of whether or not your will at the present moment desires and agrees to recognize the place you have in your Lord, and to accept it. If you are a believer, you are in Christ. If you are in Christ and wish to stay there, it is your duty to say, though it may be only for a moment, "Blessed Savior, I abide in you now; please keep me now."

It has been well said that in that little word *now* lies one of the deepest secrets of the life of faith. At the close of a conference on the spiritual life, a minister of experience rose and spoke. He said he did not know if he had learned any truth he did not know before, but he had learned how to use correctly what he already knew. He had learned that it was his privilege at each moment, whatever his surrounding circumstances might be, to say, "Jesus saves me *now*." This is the secret of rest and victory. If I can say, "Jesus is to me at this moment all that God gave Him to be—life, strength, and peace"—I only have to hold still, rest, and realize it, and for that moment I have what I need. As my faith sees how I am in Christ and takes the place in Him my Father has provided, my soul can peacefully settle down: Now I abide in Christ.

Believer, when striving to find the way to abide in Christ from moment to moment, remember that the gateway is simple: Abide in Him at this present moment. Instead of wasting effort in trying to get into a state that will last, just remember that it is Christ himself—the living, loving Lord—who alone can keep you, and is waiting to do so. Begin at once and demonstrate faith in Him for the present moment; this is the only way to be kept the next. To attain the life of permanent and perfect abiding is not ordinarily given at once as a possession for the future, it comes step by step. Avail yourself, therefore, of every opportunity to exercise the trust available at the present moment.

Each time you bow in prayer, let there first be an act of simple devotion: "Father, I am in Christ; I now abide in Him." Each time you have, in the midst of busyness, the opportunity of self-recollection, let its first involuntary act be: "I am still in Christ, abiding in Him now." Even when overtaken by sin, and your heart is all disturbed, let your first look be upward as you say: "Father, I have sinned; and yet I come—though I blush to say it—as one who is in Christ. Father, here I am! I can take no other place; of God I am in Christ; I *now* abide in Christ." Yes, Christian, in every possible circumstance, every moment of the day, the voice is calling: "Abide in Me, do it now." And even now, as you are reading this, come at once and enter into the blessed life of always abiding by doing it at once: Do it now.

In the life of David there is a beautiful passage that may help to make this thought clearer (2 Samuel 3:17–18). David had been anointed king in Judah. The other tribes still followed Ish-bosheth, Saul's son. Abner, Saul's chief captain, resolves to lead the tribes of Israel to submit to David, the God-appointed king of the whole nation. He speaks to the elders of Israel: "In time past you were seeking for David to be king over you. *Now then, do it!* For the Lord has spoken of David, saying, 'By the hand of My servant David, I will save My people Israel from the hand of the Philistines and the hand of all their enemies'" (2 Samuel 3:17–18). And they did it; they anointed David a second time to be king, now over all Israel, since they at first had only made him king over Judah (2 Samuel 5:3). This incident is a most instructive type of the way in which a soul is led to the life of entire surrender and undivided allegiance, to full abiding in Christ.

First you have *the divided kingdom*: Judah faithful to the king of God's appointment and Israel still clinging to the king of its own choosing. As a consequence, the nation was divided against itself and had no power to conquer its enemies. What a plain and clear picture of the divided heart that resides in many believers! Jesus is accepted as King in Judah, the place of the holy mount, in the inner chamber of the soul, but the surrounding territory, the everyday life, is not yet under His subjection; more than half the life is still ruled by self-will and its hosts. And so there is no real peace within and no power over one's enemies.

Then there comes *the longing desire* for a better state: "You were seeking for David to be king over you." There was a time, when David had conquered the Philistines, that Israel believed in him; but they had been led astray. Abner appeals to their own knowledge of God's will, which was that David must rule over all. So the believer, when first brought to Jesus, wanted Him to be Lord over all, and had hoped that He alone would be King. But unbelief and self-will came in, and Jesus could not assert His power over his entire life. And yet the Christian is not content. At times he longs, without daring to hope that it can be, for a better time.

Then follows *God's promise.* Abner says, "The Lord has spoken . . . By the hand of My servant David, I will save My people . . . from the hand of *all* their enemies." He appeals to

God's promise: As David had conquered the Philistines, the nearest enemy in time past, so he alone could conquer those farther off. He would save Israel from the hand of *all* their enemies. This text is a beautiful type of the promise by which the soul is now invited to trust Jesus for victory over every enemy and a life of undisturbed fellowship with Him. "The Lord has spoken"—this is our only hope. On that word rests the sure expectation (Luke 1:70–75): "As *He spoke* . . . That we should be saved from our enemies and from the hand of *all* who hate us, to perform the mercy promised to our fathers and to remember His holy covenant, the oath which He swore . . . That He would grant to us that we, being delivered out of the hand of our enemies, might serve Him without fear, in holiness and righteousness before Him all the days of our life." David reigning over every corner of the land, and leading a united and obedient people on from victory to victory: This is the promise of what Jesus can do for us, as soon as we, exercising faith in God's promise, surrender all to Him and allow our whole life to be kept abiding in Him.

"In time past you were seeking for David to be king over you," spoke Abner, and added, "Now then, do it!" *Do it now* is the message that this story brings to each one of us who longs to give Jesus unreserved supremacy. Whatever the present moment may hold, however unprepared the message finds you, however sad the divided and hopeless state of your life may be, do come and surrender—this very moment. I know that it will take time for the Lord to assert His power and arrange all within you according to His will, time to conquer your enemies and train all your powers for His service. This is not the work of a moment. But there are things that are the work of a moment—of this moment. One is your surrender of all to Jesus, your surrender of yourself entirely to live only in Him. As time goes on, and exercise has made faith stronger and brighter, that surrender may become clearer and more intelligent. But for this you cannot wait. The only way to attain it is to begin at once. *Do it now.* Surrender yourself this very moment to abide wholly, only, always in Jesus. It is the work of a moment. Remember, Christ's renewed acceptance of you is also the work of a moment. Be assured that He has you and holds you as His own, and that each new "Jesus, I do abide in you," meets with an immediate and hearty response from the Unseen One. No act of faith can be in vain. He immediately takes hold of us anew and draws us close to himself. Therefore, as often as the message comes, or the thought of it comes, Jesus says: "Abide in Me, do it at once." Each moment there is the whisper: "Do it now."

Let any Christian begin, then, and he will quickly experience how the blessing of the present moment is passed on to the next. It is the unchanging Jesus to whom he links himself; it is the power of a divine life, in its unbroken continuity, that takes possession of him. The *do it now* of the present moment—although it seems such a little thing—is nothing less than the beginning of the ever-present now, which is the mystery and the glory of eternity. Therefore, Christian, abide in Christ: *Do it now.*

Forsaking All for Him

*I have suffered the loss of all things, and count them as
rubbish, that I may gain Christ and be found in Him.*

Philippians 3:8–9

Wherever there is life, there is continual taking in and giving
out, receiving and restoring. The nourishment I take in is given
out again in the work I do; the impressions I receive, I express
in my thoughts and feelings. The one depends on the other—
the giving out ever increases the power of taking in. In the
healthy exercise of giving and taking is all the enjoyment of life.

So it is in the spiritual life too. There are Christians who
look on its blessing as consisting in the privilege of ever receiving; they do not know how the capacity for receiving is only
kept up and enlarged by continual giving up and giving out.
For it is only in the emptiness that comes from parting with
what we have that divine fullness can flow in. It was a truth our
Savior continually insisted on. When He spoke of selling all to
secure the treasure, of losing our life to find it, of the hundredfold that comes to those who forsake all, He was explaining that
self-sacrifice is the law of the kingdom for himself as well as for

His disciples. If we are really to abide in Christ, and to be found in Him—to have our life always and completely in Him—each of us in our measure must say with Paul, "I count *all things loss* for the excellence of the knowledge of Christ Jesus my Lord . . . that I may gain Christ and be found in Him" (Philippians 3: 8–9).

Let us look at what is to be forsaken and given up. First of all, there is sin. There can be no true conversion without the giving up of sin. And yet, because the young convert is often ignorant of what sin really is, of what the claims of God's holiness are, and to what extent the power of Jesus can enable us to conquer sin, the giving up of sin is at first only partial and superficial. As the Christian life grows, there comes a desire for a deeper and more entire purging out of everything that is unholy. And when the desire to abide in Christ continually, to be always found in Him, becomes strong, the soul is led to see the need of a new act of surrender, in which it accepts afresh its death to sin in Christ, and turns its back on everything that is sin. By the strength of God's Spirit, he appropriates that wonderful power of our nature by which the whole of one's future life can be gathered up and disposed of in one act of the will. In this, the believer yields himself to sin no more—to be only and wholly a servant of righteousness. He does it in the joyful assurance that every sin surrendered is gain indeed and makes room for the inflowing of the presence and the love of Christ.

After parting with unrighteousness, the believer must also give up self-righteousness. Although we contend earnestly against our own works or merits, it is often a long time before we come to really understand what it is to refuse self any place or right in the service of God. Unconsciously we allow the acts of our own mind, heart, and will to freely reign in God's presence. In prayer and worship, in Bible reading and working for God, instead of absolute dependence on the Holy Spirit's leading, self is expected to do a work it never can do. We are slow to learn the lesson "In me (that is, in my flesh) nothing good dwells" (Romans 7:18). As this truth becomes evident and we see how corruption extends to everything that is of our old nature, we understand that there can be no entire abiding in Christ without the giving up of all that is of self in religion. We must give it up to the death, and wait for the breathings of the Holy Spirit to work in us, as only He can, what is acceptable in God's sight.

We all have within us a natural life, with all the powers and gifts given to us by the Creator, which work with all the occupations and interests of the environment that surrounds us. Once you are truly converted, it is not enough that you have a sincere desire to have all these devoted to the service of the Lord. The desire is good, but it cannot teach the way or give the strength to do it acceptably. Incalculable harm has been done to the deeper spirituality of the church by the idea that when we are God's children, the using of our gifts in His service follows as a matter of course. This is not true because for this there is needed very special grace. And the way in which the grace comes is through sacrifice and surrender.

I must see how all my gifts and powers are, even though I am indeed a child of God, still defiled by sin, and under the power of the flesh. I must feel that I cannot proceed at once to use them for God's glory; I must first lay them at Christ's feet, to be accepted and cleansed by Him. *I must feel myself utterly powerless to use them correctly.* I must see that they are very dangerous to me because through them the flesh, the old nature, self, will so easily exert its power. In this conviction I must part with them, giving them entirely up to the Lord. When He has accepted them, and set His stamp upon them, I can receive them back, to hold as His property, to wait on Him for the grace to use them properly day by day, and *to have them act only under His influence.* And so experience proves it true here, too, that the path of entire consecration is the path of full salvation. Not only is what is given up received back again to become doubly our own, but the forsaking all is followed by the receiving of all. We abide in Christ more fully as we forsake all and follow Him. As I count *all things loss* for His sake, I am found in Him.

The same principle holds true for all of the legitimate occupations and possessions we have been entrusted with from God. Such were the fishnets on the Sea of Galilee, the household duties of Martha of Bethany, and the home and the friends of many of Jesus' disciples. Jesus taught them to forsake all for Him. It was no arbitrary command, but the simple application of a law in nature to the kingdom of His grace—that the more perfectly the old occupant is cast out, the more complete can be the possession of the new, and the more entire the renewal of all within.

This principle has an even deeper application. The truly spiritual gifts that are the workings of God's own Holy Spirit within us ... these surely do not need to be given up and surrendered, do they? They do indeed; the interchange of giving up and taking in is a life process and may not stop for a moment. No sooner does the believer begin to rejoice in the possession of what he has than the inflow of new grace is retarded, and stagnation threatens. It is only into the thirst of an empty soul that the streams of living waters flow. Ever thirsting is the secret of never thirsting.

Each blessed experience we receive as a gift of God must at once be returned back to Him from whom it came, in praise and love, in self-sacrifice and service; only in this way can it be restored to us again, fresh and beautiful with the bloom of heaven. This is the wonderful lesson Isaac on Mount Moriah taught us. Was he not the son of promise, the God-given life, the wonder-gift of the omnipotent One who brings to life the dead? (Romans 4:17). And yet even he had to be given up and sacrificed, that he might be received back again a thousandfold more precious than before. He serves as a type of the only-begotten Son of the Father, whose pure and holy life had to be given up before He could receive it again in resurrection power and could make His people partakers of it. A type, too, of what takes place in the life of each believer, when, instead of resting contently with past experiences or present grace, he presses on, forgetting and giving up all that is behind (Philippians 3:13), and reaches out to the fullest possible apprehension of Christ's life within.

Such surrender of all for Christ, is it a single step, the act and experience of a moment, or is it a course of daily renewal and progressive attainment? It is both. There may be a moment in the life of a believer when he gets a first glimpse, or a deeper insight, of this blessed truth, and when, made willing in the day of God's power, he does indeed gather up the whole of life yet before him into the decision of a moment, and lays himself on the altar as a living and acceptable sacrifice. Such moments have often been the blessed transition from a life of wandering and failure to a life of abiding and divine power. But even then his daily life becomes what the life must be of each one who has no such experience: the unceasing prayer for more light on the meaning of entire surrender, the ever-renewed offering up of all he has to God.

Believer, would you abide in Christ? See here the blessed path. Nature shrinks back from such self-denial and crucifixion in its rigid application to our life. But what nature does not love and cannot perform, grace will accomplish, supplying you with a life full of joy and glory. If you risk yielding yourself up to Christ your Lord, the conquering power of His incoming presence will make it joyous for you to cast out all that before was most precious.

"A hundredfold in this life" (Matthew 19:29): This word of the Master comes true to all who, with wholehearted faithfulness, accept His commands to forsake all. The blessed receiving soon makes the giving up most blessed too. And the secret of a life of close abiding will be seen to be simply this: As I give myself wholly to Christ, I find the power to take Him wholly for myself; and as I lose myself and all I have for Him, He takes me wholly for himself and gives himself wholly to me.

Through the Holy Spirit

The anointing which you have received from Him abides in you . . . and just as it has taught you, you will abide in Him.

1 John 2:27

How beautiful is the thought of a life always abiding in Christ! The longer we think of it, the more attractive it becomes. And yet how often the precious words "Abide in Me" are heard by a young disciple with a sigh! It is as if he does not understand what they mean or how such full enjoyment can be reached. He longs for someone who can make it perfectly clear, and continually reassure him that such abiding is indeed within his reach. If only this one would listen carefully to the word we have from John this day; what hope and joy it would bring! It gives us divine assurance that we have the anointing of the Holy Spirit to teach us all things, including how to abide in Christ.

Someone may say, "This word does not give me comfort; it only depresses me more. For it tells of another privilege I do not know how to enjoy. I do not understand how the teaching of the Spirit is given, where or how I can discern His voice. If the Teacher is so unknown, it is no wonder that the promise of

His teaching about abiding does not help me much."

Thoughts like these come from an error that is very common among believers. They imagine that the Spirit, in teaching them, must reveal the mysteries of the spiritual life first to their intellect, and afterward in their experience. And God's way is just the opposite of this. What holds true of all spiritual truth is especially true of abiding in Christ: *We must live and experience truth in order to know it.* Life-fellowship with Jesus is the only school for the science of heavenly things. "You do not realize now what I am doing, but later you will understand" (John 13:7 NIV) is a law of the kingdom. It is especially true of the daily cleansing of which it was first spoken, and of the daily keeping.

Receive what you do not comprehend. Submit to what you cannot understand, and accept and expect what appears to reason as a mystery. Believe what looks impossible, and walk in a way you do not know—such are the first lessons in the school of God. "*If you abide* in My word, *you will understand* the truth": in these and other words of God we are taught that there is a habit of mind and life that precedes the understanding of the truth. True discipleship consists in *first* following, and *then* knowing the Lord. The believing surrender to Christ, and submission to His Word to expect what appears most improbable, is the only way to the full blessing of knowing Him.

These principles are especially helpful in regard to the Holy Spirit's teaching. That teaching consists *in His guiding the spiritual life within us to that which God has prepared for us, without our always knowing how.* On the strength of God's promise, trusting in His faithfulness, the believer yields himself to the leading of the Holy Spirit without insisting on having it made clear to the intellect first what He is to do, but consenting to let Him do His work in the soul, and afterward come to know what He has done. Faith trusts the working of the unseen Spirit in the deep recesses of the inner life. And so the word of Christ and the gift of the Spirit are to the believer sufficient guarantee that He will be taught of the Spirit to abide in Christ. By faith he rejoices in what he does not see or feel; he knows and is confident that the blessed Spirit within is doing His work silently but surely, guiding him into a life of full abiding and unbroken communion.

The Holy Spirit is the Spirit of life in Christ Jesus; it is His work, not only to breathe, but also to always foster and strengthen, and so perfect the new life within. And in proportion as the believer yields himself in simple trust to the unseen but most certain law of the Spirit of life working within him, his faith will pass into knowledge. It will be rewarded by the Spirit's light revealing in the Word what has already been accomplished by the Spirit's power in the life.

Apply this now to the promise of the Spirit's teaching us to abide in Christ. The Holy Spirit is indeed the mighty power of God. And He comes to us from the heart of Christ as the bearer of Christ's life, the revealer and communicator of Christ himself within us. In the expression "the fellowship of the Spirit" (Philippians 2:1), we are taught what His highest work is. He is the bond of fellowship between the Father and the Son: By Him they are one. He is the bond of fellowship between all believers: By Him they are one.

Above all, He is the bond of fellowship between Christ and individual believers; He is the life-sap through which Vine and branch grow into real and living oneness: By Him we are one.

And we can be assured of it, that if we believe in His presence and working, if we are careful not to grieve Him because we know that He is in us, and if we wait and pray to be filled with Him, He will teach us how to abide. First guiding our will to a wholehearted clinging to Christ, then energizing our faith into ever-growing confidence and expectation, then breathing into our hearts a peace and joy that pass understanding, He teaches us to abide. Then coming through the heart and life into the understanding, He helps us grasp the truth—not as mere thought, but as the truth which is in Christ Jesus. It comes as a reflection into the mind of the light of what He has already made a reality in the life. "In him was life, and that life was the light of men" (John 1:4 NIV).

In view of such teaching, it is clear that if we would have the Spirit guide us into the abiding life, our first need is quiet, restful faith. Amid all the questions and difficulties that may come up in connection with our striving to abide in Christ, all the longing we may sometimes feel to have a seasoned Christian to help us, and the frequent painful consciousness of failure, ignorance, and helplessness, we need to remember with blessed confidence: *We have the anointing of the Holy One to teach us to abide in Him.* "The anointing which you have received from Him abides in you ... and just as it has taught you, you will abide in Him." Make this teaching of His about abiding a matter of faith.

Believe that as surely as you have Christ, you have His Spirit too. Believe that He will do His work with power, if only you do not hinder Him. Believe that He is working, even when you cannot recognize it. Believe that He will work mightily if you ask this from the Father. *It is impossible to live the life of full abiding without being full of the Holy Spirit*; believe that the fullness of the Spirit is your daily privilege. Be sure to take time in prayer to dwell before the throne of God and the Lamb, from which flows the river of the water of life (Revelation 22:1). It is *there, and only there,* that you can be filled with the Spirit. Cultivate carefully the habit of daily, continually honoring Him by quiet, restful confidence that He is doing His work within. Let faith in His indwelling make you jealous of whatever could grieve Him—the spirit of the world or the actions of self and the flesh. Let your faith seek its nourishment in the Word and all it says of the Spirit, His power, His comfort, and His work.

Above all, let faith in the Spirit's indwelling lead you to look away to Jesus. As we have received the anointing of *Him*, it comes in ever-stronger flow from Him as we are occupied with Christ alone. Christ is the Anointed One. As we look up to Him, the holy anointing comes, the "precious oil poured on the head, running down on the beard, running down on Aaron's beard, down upon the collar of his robes" (Psalm 133:2 NIV). It is faith in Jesus that brings the anointing; then the anointing leads to Jesus and enables us to abide in Him alone.

Believer, abide in Christ, by the power of the Spirit. What do you think? Should such abiding be a fear or a burden? Surely not! If we only knew the graciousness of our Holy Comforter, and the blessing of wholly yielding ourselves to His leading, we would experience the divine comfort of having such a teacher to secure our abiding in Christ. The Holy Spirit was given for this one purpose: that *the glorious redemption and life in Christ might be given and communicated to us with divine power.* We have the Holy Spirit to make the living Christ, in all His saving power and complete victory over sin, ever present within us. It is this that makes Him the Comforter; with Him we need never mourn an absent Christ.

Let us therefore, as often as we read, meditate, or pray about abiding in Christ, count on it as a settled thing that we have the Spirit of God himself within us, teaching, guiding, and working. The Holy Spirit is always at work with secret but divine power in the trusting soul that does not hinder His work by its unbelief. For this reason, we can rejoice in the confidence that we will succeed in our desires to abide in Him if we will only let the Holy Spirit do the work in us.

In Stillness of Soul

*In repentance and rest is your salvation, in quietness
and trust is your strength.*

Isaiah 30:15 (NIV)

Rest in the Lord, and wait patiently for Him.

Psalm 37:7

Truly my soul silently waits for God.

Psalm 62:1

There is a view of the Christian life that regards it as a sort of partnership, in which God and man each have to do their part. It admits that there is little that man can do, and even that little is defiled with sin; still, the view holds, man must do his utmost; only then can he expect God to do His part. To those who think this way, it is extremely difficult to understand what Scripture means when it speaks of our being still and doing nothing, of our resting and waiting to see the salvation of God. It appears to them a perfect contradiction when we speak of this quietness and ceasing from all effort as the secret of the most productive activity of man. And yet this is just what Scripture does teach.

The explanation of the apparent mystery is to be found in this: When God and man are spoken of as working together, it is not in the usual sense of a partnership between two partners who each contribute out of their individual reserves their share to a mutual project. The relationship between a believer and Christ is a very different one. Here, cooperation is founded on subordination. As Jesus was entirely dependent on the Father for all His words and all His works, so the believer can do nothing of himself. What he can do of himself is altogether sinful. He must therefore cease entirely from his own doing and wait for the working of God in him. As he ceases from self-effort, faith assures him that God is working in him to complete the work; what God does is to renew, sanctify, and awaken all his energies to their highest power.

So as the believer yields himself as a truly passive instrument in the hand of God, and works with renewed confidence in God's almighty power rather than his own, in that proportion will he experience the deepest possible expression of the Christian life. Passivity does not mean inactivity; it means that as we live out our Christian responsibilities, we do not trust in our own strength but in God's at work within us.

Among the lessons to be learned of those who are studying the blessed art of abiding in Christ, there is none more needful and more profitable than cultivating stillness of soul. In it alone can we produce a teachable spirit, to which the Lord will reveal His secrets. To the meek He shows His ways. This spirit was exhibited so beautifully by three women in the New Testament. It was evident in Jesus' mother, whose only answer to the most wonderful revelation ever made to a human being was, "I am the Lord's servant, May it be to me as you have said" (Luke 1:38 NIV); and as mysteries multiplied around her, it is written of her: "Mary kept all these things and pondered them in her heart" (Luke 2:19). In Mary of Bethany, who "sat at Jesus' feet and heard His word" (Luke 10:39), and who showed in anointing Him for His burial how she had understood the mystery of His death better than His disciples had, we also see this spirit of meekness. She wanted to be still and learn from the One who had the words of life. We also see a meek and quiet spirit in the sinful woman who sought the Lord in the house of the Pharisee, with tears that spoke more than words (Luke 7:37–38). It is *a soul silent before God* that is best prepared for knowing Jesus, and for holding on to the blessings He bestows. It is when the soul is hushed in silent awe and worship before the Holy Presence revealed within that the still, small voice of the blessed Spirit will be heard.

Therefore, beloved Christian, as often as you seek to better understand the blessed mystery of abiding in Christ, let this be your first thought: "My soul, *wait silently* for God alone; for my expectation is from Him" (Psalm 62:5). Do you hope to realize the wondrous union with the Heavenly Vine? Then know that flesh and blood cannot reveal it to you, but only the Father in heaven. You only have to acknowledge your own ignorance and impotence; the Father will delight to give you the teaching of the Holy Spirit. If your ear is open, and your thoughts are brought into subjection, and your heart is prepared in silence to wait upon God and to hear what He speaks, then He will reveal to you His secrets.

One of the first secrets revealed will be deeper insight into the truth that as you sink low before Him in nothingness and helplessness, in a silence and stillness of soul that seeks to catch the faintest whisper of His love, teachings will come to you that you never heard before because of the rush and noise of your own thoughts and efforts. You will learn how your best work is to listen, hear, and believe what He promises; to watch, wait, and see what He does; and then, by faith, worship, and obedience, to yield yourself to the One who works mightily in you.

One would think that no message could be more beautiful or welcome than this: that we may rest and be quiet, and that our God will work for us and in us. And yet how far this is from being the case! How slow many are to learn that quietness is blessing, that quietness is strength, that quietness is the source of the highest activity—the secret of all true abiding in Christ! Let us try to learn it and to watch out for whatever interferes with it. The dangers that threaten the soul's rest are many.

There is a depleting of energy that comes from entering needlessly and too deeply into the interests of this world. Every one of us has his divine calling; and within the circle pointed out by God himself, interest in our work and its surroundings is a duty. But even here the Christian needs to be watchful and sober-minded. We need a holy self-control in regard to things not absolutely imposed upon us by God. If abiding in Christ is really our first aim, we must beware of all needless entertainment. We must watch even in lawful and necessary things against the wondrous power these have to keep the soul so occupied that there remains little power or zest for fellowship with God. Then there is the restlessness and worry from care and anxiety about earthly things; these eat away the life of trust and keep the soul like a troubled sea. There the gentle whispers of the Holy Comforter cannot be heard.

No less hurtful is the spirit of fear and distrust in spiritual things; with its apprehensions, it never really hears what God has to say. Above all, though, is the unrest that comes from seeking in our own way and in our own strength the spiritual blessing that comes only from above. *The heart occupied with its own plans and efforts for doing God's will and securing the blessing of abiding in Jesus will fail continually.* God's work is hindered by our interference. He can do His work perfectly only when the soul ceases from its work. He will do His work mightily in the soul that honors Him by expecting Him to work both in intent and fulfillment.

Last of all, even when the soul seeks to enter the way of faith, there is the impatience of the flesh, which forms its judgment of the life and progress of the soul not according to the divine but a human standard.

In dealing with all this, and so much more, blessed is the man who learns the lesson of stillness, and fully accepts God's Word: "In quietness and confidence shall be your strength." Each time he listens to the word of the Father, or asks the Father to listen to his words, he does not dare to begin his Bible reading or prayer without first pausing and waiting, until the soul is hushed in the presence of the Eternal Majesty. Under a sense of the Divine nearness, the soul, feeling how self is always ready to assert itself and intrude even into the holiest of all with its thoughts and efforts, yields itself in a quiet act of self-surrender to the teaching and working of the Holy Spirit. It is still and waits in holy silence, until all is calm and ready to receive the revelation of the divine will and presence. Its reading and prayer then become a waiting on God with ear and heart open, cleansed to receive fully only what He says.

"Abide in Christ!" Let no one think that he can do this if he does not have his daily quiet time, his seasons of meditation and waiting on God. In these a habit of soul must be cultivated, in which the believer goes out into the world and its distractions with the peace of God that surpasses all understanding, guarding the heart and mind (Philippians 4:7). It is in such a calm and restful soul that the life of faith can take root deeply, the Holy Spirit can give His blessed teaching, and the Father can accomplish His glorious work.

May each one of us learn every day to say, "Truly my soul silently waits for God." And may every feeling of difficulty in attaining this only cause us to look to Him and trust the One whose presence makes even a storm to be calm. Cultivate quietness as a means to abiding in Christ, and expect the ever-deepening quietness and calm of heaven in the soul as the fruit of abiding in Him.

In Affliction and Trial

Every branch that bears fruit He prunes,
that it may bear more fruit.

John 15:2

In the whole plant world there is not a tree to be found that so suits the image of man in his relationship to God as the vine. No other plant has fruit and juice that are so full of spirit, so alive and stimulating. But there is also none that has such a natural tendency toward evil, that is, growth that loves to run into wood that is utterly worthless except for the fire. Of all plants, the vine most needs the pruning knife to be used unsparingly and unceasingly. Also, none is so dependent on cultivation and training. But even with all these problems, no other plant yields a richer reward to the Vinedresser. In His wonderful parable, the Savior refers to this need of pruning the vine, and the blessing it brings. In this dark world, often so full of suffering and sorrow for believers, we can take comfort in His words about pruning, knowing that He means it for our good.

What treasures of teaching and comfort to the bleeding branch in its hour of trial: "Every branch that bears fruit *He prunes*, that it may bear more fruit." This is how He prepares

His people, who are prone when trial comes to be shaken in their confidence and to be moved away from abiding in Christ; in each affliction we need to hear the voice of a messenger that encourages us to abide even closer. Yes, believer, especially in times of trial, abide in Christ.

Abide in Christ! This is *the Father's object* in sending the trial. In a storm the tree puts down deeper roots into the soil; in a hurricane the inhabitants of the house stay inside and rejoice in its shelter. Through suffering the Father leads us to enter more deeply into the love of Christ. Our hearts are continually prone to wander from Him; prosperity and enjoyment all too easily satisfy us, dull our spiritual perception, and make us unfit for full communion with God. It is an unspeakable mercy that the Father comes with His affliction and makes the world around us dark and unattractive. This leads us to feel more deeply our sinfulness, and for a time we lose our joy in what was becoming so threatening to our spiritual life. He does this in the hope that when we have found our rest in Christ in time of trouble, we will learn to choose abiding in Him as our best option. Then when the affliction is removed, His hope for us is that we will have grown more firmly in Him, so that in prosperity He will still be our only joy. He has set His heart on this to the point that although He has no pleasure in afflicting us, He will not hold back even the most painful correction if He can thereby guide His beloved child to come home and abide in the beloved Son. Christian, pray for grace to see in every trouble, small or great, the Father pointing you to Jesus, and saying, "Abide in Him."

Abide in Christ; in this way you will become *partaker of all the rich blessings God designed for you* in the affliction. The purposes of God's wisdom will become clear to you, your assurance of His unchangeable love will become stronger, and the power of His Spirit will fulfill in you the promise "God disciplines us for our good, that we may share in his holiness" (Hebrews 12:10 NIV). Abide in Christ, and your cross becomes the means of fellowship with His Cross, providing access into its mysteries—the mystery of the curse that He bore for you, of the death to sin in which you partake with Him, and of the love in which, as sympathizing High Priest, He descended into all your sorrows. Abide in Christ; for by conforming to your blessed Lord in His sufferings, a deeper experience of the reality and the tenderness of His love will be yours.

Abide in Christ; in the fiery furnace, one like the Son of Man will be seen as never before and the burning away of the dross and the refining of the gold will be accomplished. Then Christ's own likeness will be reflected in you. If you abide in Christ, the power of the flesh will be put to death, and the impatience and self-will of the old nature will be humbled to make room for the meekness and gentleness of Christ. A believer may pass through a lot of affliction and, sadly, receive little blessing from it all. Abiding in Christ is the secret to receiving all the benefits that the Father meant for us to have from such experiences.

Abide in Christ; in Him you will find *sure and abundant consolation.* Comfort is often the first priority with the afflicted, and the profit of the affliction only of secondary interest. But our heavenly Father loves us so much that though our real and abiding profit is His first object of interest, He does not forget to comfort us too. When He comforts, it is that He may turn the believer's aching heart to Christ to receive the blessing of fellowship with Him. When He refuses to comfort us, His object is still the same. It is in making us partakers of His holiness that true comfort comes. The Holy Spirit is the Comforter, not only because He can suggest comforting thoughts of God's love, but far more, because He makes us holy and brings us into close union with Christ and the Father.

In Christ, the heart of the Father is revealed, and there can be no higher comfort than to rest in the Father's arms. *In Him* the fullness of the Divine Love is revealed, combined with the tenderness of a mother's compassion—and what can comfort like this? *In Him* you see a thousand times more given to you than you have lost; see how God only took from you so that you might have room to take from Him what is so much better. *In Him* suffering is consecrated and becomes the foretaste of eternal glory; in suffering the Spirit of God and of glory rests on us. Believer, would you have comfort in affliction? Then abide in Christ.

If you want to *bear more fruit* you must abide in Him. Not a vine is planted but the owner thinks of the fruit, and the fruit only. Other trees may be planted for ornament, for shade, or for wood, but the vine is planted *only for the fruit*. And of each vine the vinedresser is continually asking how it can bring forth more fruit, much fruit. If we can learn to abide in Christ in times of affliction, we will bear more fruit. The deeper experience of Christ's tenderness and the Father's love will urge you to live to His glory. Another benefit of surrender of self and self-will in suffering is that it will prepare you to sympathize with the misery of others; the softening that comes from such experiences will enable you to become, as Jesus was, the servant of all. The thought of the Father's desire for fruit in the pruning will help you to yield yourself afresh, and more than ever, to

Him, and to say that now you have but one object in life: making known and conveying His wonderful love to others. You will learn the art of forgetting self, and, even in affliction, using this separation from ordinary life to plead for the welfare of others. When you see affliction coming, meet it in Christ; when it has come, feel that you are more in Christ than in the affliction, for He is closer to you than affliction ever can be; and when it is passing, still abide in Him. Let the one thought of the Savior, as He speaks of the pruning, and the one desire of the Father, as He does the pruning, be yours: "Every branch that bears fruit He prunes, that it may bear *more fruit.*"

In this way, your times of affliction become your times of choicest blessing—preparation for rich fruitfulness. Led into closer fellowship with the Son of God, and a deeper experience of His love and grace, you are established in the blessed confidence that He and you belong entirely to each other. You will find that you are more completely satisfied with Him and more wholly given up to Him than ever before. With your own will crucified, and your heart brought into deeper harmony with God's will, you will be a cleansed vessel that is suitable for the Master's use, prepared for every good work (2 Timothy 3:17).

True believer, try to learn this important truth, that in affliction your first, your only, calling that will be blessed is to abide in Christ. Spend much time with Him alone. Beware of the comfort and the distractions that friends so often bring. Let Jesus Christ be your chief companion and comforter. Delight yourself in the assurance that closer union with Him and more abundant fruit through Him are sure to be the results of trial because it is the Vinedresser himself who is doing the pruning. He will ensure the fulfillment of the desire of the soul that yields itself lovingly to His work.

That You May Bear Much Fruit

He who abides in Me, and I in him, bears much fruit; By this My Father is glorified, that you bear much fruit.

John 15:5, 8

We all know what fruit is—the produce of the branch that refreshes and nourishes men. The fruit is not for the branch, but for those who come to carry it away. As soon as the fruit is ripe, the branch gives it up, to begin again its work of benevolence, and to prepare its fruit for another season. A fruit-bearing tree does not live for itself, but entirely for those to whom its fruit brings refreshment and life. And so the branch's whole existence is for the sake of the fruit, while its object and glory is to make the heart of the vinedresser glad.

What a beautiful image of the believer who is abiding in Christ! He not only grows in strength as his union with the Vine becomes progressively surer and firmer but he also bears fruit, much fruit to God's glory. He has the power to offer to others something to eat and by which they may live. Among all who surround him he becomes like a tree of life, of which they can taste and be refreshed. He is in his circle a center of life and blessing simply because he abides in Christ; he receives from Him the Spirit and the life that he can then impart to others. If you would bless others, learn to abide in Christ; and if you do abide, you will indeed be a blessing. As surely as the branch abiding in a fruitful vine bears fruit, so surely, *much more surely*, will a soul abiding in Christ with His fullness of blessing be made a blessing.

The reason for this is easily understood. If Christ, the Heavenly Vine, has taken the believer as a branch, then He has pledged himself, in the very nature of things, to supply the sap, spirit, and nourishment to make it bear fruit. The soul needs to concern itself with only one thing—to abide closely, fully, and entirely in Him. Christ will give the fruit. He works all that is needed to make the believer a blessing.

Abiding in Him, you receive from Him *His Spirit of love and compassion toward sinners*, which makes you want to see them blessed. By nature the heart is full of selfishness. Even in the believer, his own salvation and happiness is too often his only object. But abiding in Jesus, you come into contact with His infinite love, and its fire begins to burn within your heart; you see the beauty of love; you learn to look upon loving, serving, and saving your fellowmen as the highest privilege a disciple of Jesus can have. Abiding in Christ, your heart learns to feel the wretched condition of sinners still in darkness, and what dishonor is done to God by their alienation from Him. With Christ you begin to bear the burden of souls, the burden of sins not your own. As you are more closely united to Him, some measure of that passion for souls that urged Him to Calvary begins to breathe within you, and you are ready to follow His footsteps, to forsake the heaven of your own happiness and devote your life to win the souls Christ has taught you to love. The very spirit of the Vine is love, and this spirit of love streams into the branch that abides in Him.

The desire to be a blessing is just the beginning. As you begin to work, you quickly become conscious of your own weakness and the difficulties in your way. You realize that souls are not saved at your bidding. You become discouraged, and are tempted to relax your effort. But by abiding in Christ you receive *new courage and strength for the work.* Believing what Christ teaches, that it is *He* who *through you* will give His blessing to the world, you understand that you are only a weak instrument through which the hidden power of Christ does its work. You find that His strength may be perfected and made glorious in your weakness.

It is a great step when the believer fully consents to his own weakness, and the abiding consciousness of it, and so works faithfully on, fully assured that his Lord *is working* through him. He rejoices that the excellence of the power is of God, and not of him (2 Corinthians 4:7). Realizing his oneness with his Lord, he no longer considers his own weakness, but counts on the power of Him whose hidden workings make all the difference. It is this secret assurance that gives brightness to his look, a gentle firmness to his tone, and perseverance to all his efforts, all effective means of influencing those he is seeking to win. He goes forth in the spirit of one who knows that victory is assured; for this is the victory that overcomes, even our faith (1 John 5:4). He no longer considers it humility to say that God cannot bless his unworthy efforts. He claims and expects a blessing because it is not he, but Christ within, that will accomplish it.

The great secret of abiding in Christ is the deep conviction that we are nothing, and He is everything. As this is learned, it no longer seems strange to believe that our weakness need not be a hindrance to His saving power. The believer who yields himself wholly to Christ for service in the spirit of a simple, childlike trust will most certainly bear much fruit. He will not fear to claim his share in the wonderful promise: "He who believes in Me, the works that I do he will do also; and *greater works* than these he will do, because I go to My Father" (John 14:12). He no longer thinks that He cannot have a blessing or be fruitful in order that he may be kept humble. He sees that the most heavily laden branches bow down the lowest! Abiding in Christ, he has agreed that, as is true in the arrangement between all vines and branches, any fruit will be to the glory of the Heavenly Vinedresser alone.

Let us learn two lessons. If we are abiding in Jesus, let us begin to work. Let us first seek to influence those around us in daily life. Let us accept distinctly and joyfully our holy calling, that we are even now to live as servants of the love of Jesus to our fellowmen. Our daily life must have for its object the making of an impression favorable to Jesus. When you look at the branch, you see at once the likeness to the Vine. We must live so that something of the holiness and the gentleness of Jesus may shine out in us. We must live to represent Him. As was the case with Him while on earth, the life must prepare the way for the teaching.

What the church and the world both need is this: men and women full of the Holy Spirit and of love, who, as living examples of the grace and power of Christ, witness for Him and for His power on behalf of those who believe in Him. Living so, with our hearts longing to have Jesus glorified in the souls He is seeking after, let us offer ourselves to Him for practical expressions of mercy. There is work to be done in our own homes. There is work among the sick, the poor, and the outcast. There is work in a hundred different paths that the Spirit of Christ opens up through those who allow themselves to be led by Him. There is work perhaps for us in ways that have not yet been opened up by others. Abiding in Christ, let us work. Let us work not like those who are content if they simply follow the expectations of our society and take some share in Christian work. No; let us work as those who are growing more like Christ because they are abiding in Him, and who, like Him, count the work of winning souls to the Father the very joy and glory of heaven begun on earth.

The second lesson is: If you work, abide in Christ. This is one of the blessings of work if done in the right spirit—it will deepen your union with your blessed Lord. It will discover your weakness and throw you back on His strength. It will stir you to pray more; and in prayer for others is the time when the soul, forgetful of itself, unconsciously grows deeper into Christ. Prayer will make clearer to you the true nature of branch-life, its absolute dependence, and at the same time its glorious sufficiency independent of all else, because it is only dependent on Jesus.

If you work, abide in Christ. There are temptations and dangers. Work for Christ has sometimes drawn believers away from Christ and taken the place of fellowship with Him. Work can sometimes present a form of godliness without the power.

As you work, abide in Christ. Let a living faith in Christ working in you be the secret spring of all your work; this will inspire in you both humility and courage. Let the Holy Spirit of Jesus dwell in you as the Spirit of His tender compassion and His divine power. Abide in Christ, and offer every part of your nature freely and unreservedly to Him to sanctify it for himself. If Jesus Christ is really to work through us, it will require an entire consecration of ourselves to Him that is renewed daily. But we understand now, this is what abiding in Christ means; this is what constitutes our highest privilege and happiness. To be a branch bearing much fruit—nothing less, nothing more—may this be our only joy.

So Will You Have Power
in Prayer

If ye abide in Me, and My words abide in you, you shall ask
what you desire, and it shall be done for you.

John 15:7

Prayer is both one of the means and one of the fruits of union with Christ. As a means it is of great importance. All the things of faith, all the pleadings of desire, all the yearnings after a fuller surrender, all the confessions of shortcoming and of sin, all the exercises in which the soul gives up self and clings to Christ, find their utterance in prayer. In each meditation on abiding in Christ, as some new feature of what Scripture teaches concerning this blessed life is understood, the first impulse of the believer is to look up to the Father and pour out his heart, to ask Him for the full understanding and the full possession of what has been revealed in the Word. And it is the believer who is not content with this spontaneous expression of his hope, but who takes time in secret prayer to wait until he has received what he has seen, who will really grow strong in Christ.

However weak the soul's first abiding, its prayer will be heard, and it will find prayer one of the best means of abiding more abundantly.

But it is not so much as a means but as a fruit of abiding that the Savior mentions it in the parable of the Vine. He does not think of prayer as we too often do—exclusively as a means of getting blessing for ourselves. Rather, He sees prayer as one of the primary channels of influence by which, through us as workers together with God, the blessings of Christ's redemption are dispensed to the world. He sets before himself and us the glory of the Father, in the extension of His kingdom, as the object for which we have been made branches; and He assures us that if we will only abide in Him, we will be Israels, having power with God and man. Ours will be the effectual, fervent prayer of a righteous man, availing much, like Elijah's prayer for ungodly Israel (James 5:16–18). Such prayer will be the fruit of our abiding in Him and the means of bearing much fruit.

To the Christian who is not abiding completely in Jesus, the difficulties connected with prayer are often so great that they rob him of the comfort and the strength it could bring. Under the guise of humility, he asks how one so unworthy could expect to have influence with the Holy One. He thinks of God's sovereignty, His perfect wisdom and love, and cannot see how his prayer can really have any distinct effect. He prays, but it is more because he cannot rest without prayer than from a loving faith that the prayer will be heard. But what a blessed release from such questions and perplexities is given to the soul who is truly abiding in Christ! He realizes more and more how it is in real spiritual unity with Christ that we are accepted and heard. The union with the Son of God is a life union; we are indeed one with Him—our prayer ascends as His prayer. It is because we abide in Him that we can ask what we desire and it is given to us.

There are many reasons why this must be so. One is that abiding in Christ, and having His words abiding in us, teaches us to pray *in accordance with the will of God*. As we abide in Christ our self-will is kept down, and the thoughts and wishes of the old nature are brought into captivity to the thoughts and wishes of Christ; like-mindedness to Christ grows in us and as a result all our works and desires come into harmony with His. There is deep and frequent heart-searching to see whether the surrender is complete, fervent prayer to the heart-searching Spirit that nothing may be kept back. Everything is yielded to the power of His life in us so that it may exercise its sanctifying influence even on ordinary wishes and desires. His Holy Spirit breathes through our whole being. Without our being conscious how, our desires, as the breathings of the divine life, are brought into conformity with the divine will, and are fulfilled. Abiding in Christ renews and sanctifies the will; we then ask what we will, and it is given to us.

In close connection with this is the thought that abiding in Christ teaches the believer in prayer *only to seek the glory of God*. In promising to answer prayer, Christ's one thought (see John 14:13) is this, "that the Father may be glorified in the Son." In His intercession on earth (John 17), this was His one desire and plea; in His intercession in heaven, it is still His chief object. As the believer abides in Christ, the Savior breathes this desire into him. The thought *only the glory of God* becomes more and more the keynote of the life hidden in Christ. At first this subdues, quiets, and makes the soul almost afraid to entertain a wish, lest it should not be to the Father's glory. But when His glory has finally been accepted, and everything yielded to it, it comes with mighty power to enlarge the heart and open it to the vast possibilities in the area of God's glory. Abiding in Christ, the soul learns not only to desire but also to spiritually discern what will be for God's glory. One of the first conditions of acceptable prayer is fulfilled in it when, as the fruit of its union with Christ, the whole mind is brought into harmony with that of the Son as He said, "Father, glorify Your name" (John 12:28).

Abiding in Christ, we can freely use *the name of Christ.* Asking in the name of another means that person has authorized me and sent me to ask. The person doing the asking wants the favor done for him. Believers often try to think of the name of Jesus and His merits, and to talk themselves into the faith that they will be heard, while they painfully acknowledge how little faith they have in His name. They are not living wholly in Jesus' name. This is obvious because it is only when they begin to pray that they want to take up His name and use it. But this is not what Scripture teaches. The promise "Whatever you ask in My name" (John 14:13) cannot be separated from the command "Whatever you do in word or deed, *do all in the name* of the Lord Jesus" (Colossians 3:17).

If the name of Christ is to be at my disposal, so that I may have the full command of it for all I desire, it must be because I first put myself at His disposal, so that He has free and full command of me. It is abiding in Christ that gives us the right and power to use His name with confidence. To Christ, the Father refuses nothing. Abiding in Christ, I come to the Father as one with Him. His righteousness, as well as His Spirit, is in me; the Father sees the Son in me, and gives me my petition. It is not—as so many think—by a sort of imputed act that the Father looks upon us as if we were in Christ, even when we are not, in fact, in Him. No; the Father wants to *see* us living in Him; in this way our prayer really will have power to prevail. Abiding in Christ not only renews the will to pray in the right spirit but also secures the full power of His merits to us.

Abiding in Christ also works in us *the faith that can obtain an answer.* "According to your faith let it be to you" (Matthew 9:29); this is one of the laws of the kingdom. "Believe that you receive them, and you will have them" (Mark 11:24). This faith rests upon and is rooted in the Word, but is something infinitely higher than the mere logical conclusion: God has promised, therefore I will obtain. No; faith, as a spiritual act, depends upon the words abiding in us as living power, and so upon the state of the whole inner life. Without fasting and prayer (Mark 9:29), without humility and a spiritual mind (John 5:44), without wholehearted obedience (1 John 3:22), there cannot be this living faith. But as the soul abides in Christ, and grows into the consciousness of its union with Him, and sees how it is only Jesus who makes its petition acceptable, it dares to claim an answer because it knows that it is one with Him. It was by faith it learned to abide in Him; as the fruit of that faith, it rises to even greater faith in all that God has promised to be and to do. It learns to breathe its prayers in deep, quiet, confident assurance: We know we have the petition we ask of Him.

Abiding in Christ keeps us in the place where *the answer can be given.* Some believers pray earnestly for blessing, but when God comes and looks for them to bless them, they are not to be found. They did not realize that the blessing must not only be asked, but also waited for, and received in prayer. Abiding in Christ is the place for receiving answers. If the answer came outside of Him it would be dangerous in that we would only spend it on our own pleasures (James 4:3). Many of the richest answers—for spiritual grace, for example, or for power to work and to bless others—can only come in the form of a larger experience with God in what He makes Christ to us. The fullness is *in Him*; abiding in Him is the condition for power in prayer because the answer is treasured up and given in Him.

Believer, abide in Christ, for there in the abiding is the school of prayer—mighty, effectual, answered prayer. Abide in Him, and you will learn what to so many is a mystery: *The secret of the prayer of faith is the life of faith*—the life that abides in Christ alone.

Continue in His Love

As the Father loved Me, I also have loved you;
continue in My love.

John 15:9

Blessed Lord, enlighten our eyes to see clearly the glory of this wondrous word. Open to our meditation the secret chamber of your love, so that our souls may enter in, and find there their everlasting dwelling place. How else will we comprehend a love "which passes knowledge" (Ephesians 3:19)?

Before the Savior speaks the word that invites us to continue in His love, He first tells us what that love is. What He says of it gives power to His invitation and makes the thought of not accepting it an impossibility: "As the Father loved me, I also have loved you!"

"As the Father loved me" . . . How can we rightly comprehend this love? Lord, teach us. God is love; love is His very being. Love is not an attribute, but the very essence of His nature, the center around which all His glorious attributes revolve. It is because He is love that He is the Father, and that there is a Son. Love needs an object to give itself away to, in whom it can lose itself, with whom it can make itself one. Because God is love, there must be a Father and a Son. The love of the Father to the Son is that divine passion that finds delight in the Son and declares of Him, "This is My beloved Son, in whom I am well-pleased" (Matthew 3:17). Divine love is a burning fire; in all its intensity and infinity it has but one object and one joy: the only begotten Son. When we gather together all the attributes of God—His infinity, His perfection, His immensity, His majesty, His omnipotence—and consider them as only rays of the glory of His love, we still fail to grasp what that love must be. It is a love that passes knowledge.

And yet this love of God to His Son must serve as the glass in which you are to learn how Jesus loves you. As one of His redeemed ones you are His delight, and all His desire is to you, with the longing of a love that is stronger than death, and which many waters cannot quench. His heart yearns for you, seeking your fellowship and your love. If it were needed, He would die again to possess you. As the Father loved the Son, and could not live without Him—this is how Jesus loves you. His life is bound up in yours; you are to Him inexpressibly more indispensable and precious than you can ever know. You are one with Him. "As the Father loved me, I also have loved you." What love!

It is an eternal love. From before the foundation of the world—God's Word teaches us this—the purpose had been formed that Christ should be the head of His church, that He should have a body in which His glory could be shown. In that eternity He loved and longed for those who had been given to Him by the Father; and when He came and told His disciples that He loved them, it was not with a love of earth and of time, but with the love of eternity. And it is with that same infinite love that His eye still rests upon each of us here seeking to abide in Him. In each expression of that love there is the very power of eternity. "I have loved you with an everlasting love" (Jeremiah 31:3).

It is also a perfect love. It gives all, and holds nothing back. "The Father loves the Son, and has given all things into His hand" (John 3:35). And in the same way, Jesus loves His own; all He has is theirs. When it was needed, He sacrificed His throne and crown for you; He did not count His own life and blood too dear to give for you. His righteousness, His Spirit, His glory, even His throne—all are yours. This love holds nothing back, but, in a manner that no human mind can grasp, makes you one with itself. O wondrous love! For Christ to love us even as the Father loved Him, and to offer us this love as our everyday dwelling is truly amazing.

His is a gentle and most tender love. As we think of the love of the Father to the Son, we see in the Son everything so infinitely worthy of that love. But when we think of Christ's love to us, there is nothing but sin and unworthiness to meet the eye. And the question inevitably comes: How can that love within the heart of God with all His perfections be compared to the love that rests on sinners? Can it indeed be the same love? Praise be to God, we know it is so. The nature of love is always the same, however different the objects of it might be. Christ knows of no other law of love but that with which His Father loved Him. Our sinfulness only serves to call out more distinctly the beauty of His love, such love as could not be seen even in heaven. With tender compassion He bows to our weakness, with inconceivable patience He bears with our slowness, with the gentlest loving-kindness He meets our fears and our failures. It is the love of the Father to the Son, beautified and glorified in its condescension, in its exquisite adaptation to our needs.

It is an unchangeable love. "Having loved His own who were in the world, He loved them to the end" (John 13:1). "The mountains shall depart and the hills be removed, but My kindness shall not depart from you" (Isaiah 54:10). The promise with which love begins its work in the soul is this: "I will not leave you until I have done what I have spoken to you" (Genesis 28:15). And just as our wretchedness was what first drew it to us, so our sin, which so often grieves His love, and which may cause us to fear and doubt, is only a new motive for love to hold us even more tightly. And why is this so? We can give no other reason than this: "As the Father loved me, I also have loved you."

And now we need to look at the implications of this tremendous love. For God's love suggests the *motive*, the *measure*, and the *means* by which we can yield ourselves to wholly abide in Him.

This love definitely supplies a motive. Only look and see how this love stands, pleads, and prays. Gaze on the divine form, the eternal glory, the heavenly beauty, and the tenderly pleading gentleness of Crucified Love as it stretches out its pierced hands and asks, "Will you not abide with Me? Will you not come and abide in Me?" It points you up to the eternity of love from which it came to seek you. It points you to the Cross and all it has carried to prove the reality of its affection, and to win you for itself. It reminds you of all it has promised to do for you, if you will only yield yourself unreservedly into its arms. It asks you if, so far as you have come to dwell with it and taste its blessing, it has done well by you. And with a divine authority, mingled with such inexpressible tenderness that one might almost think he heard the tone of reproach in it, it says, "Soul, as the Father has loved me, I also have loved you: continue in My love." Surely there can be but one answer to such pleading: Lord Jesus Christ, here I am! From now on your love will be the only home of my soul; in your love alone will I abide.

His love is not only the motive but also the measure of our surrender to abide in it. Love gives all, but also asks all. It does so not because it begrudges us what has been given, but because without this it cannot get possession of us to fill us with itself. In the love of the Father and the Son, it was so. In the love of Jesus to us, it was so. In our entering into His love to abide there, it must be so; our surrender to it must have no other measure than its surrender to us. If only we could understand how the love that calls us has infinite riches and fullness of joy for us, and that what we give up for its sake will be rewarded a hundredfold in this life! It is love with height and depth and length and breadth that passes knowledge (Ephesians 3:18–19)! If we could grasp even a part of its knowledge, all thought of sacrifice or surrender would pass away, and our souls would be filled with wonder at the unspeakable privilege of being loved with such love, of being allowed to come and abide in it forever.

And if doubt again suggests the question: But is it possible that I can always abide in His love? Then listen how such love itself supplies the only means for abiding in Him: It is faith in that love that will enable us to abide in it. If this love is so divine, such an intense and burning passion, then surely I can depend on it to keep me in its grasp. Surely all my unworthiness and frailty can be no hindrance to such love. If this love, being divine, has infinite power at its command, I surely have a right to trust that it is stronger than my weakness and that with its almighty arm it will hold me in its arms and allow me to wander no more. I see how this is the one thing my God requires of me. Treating me as a reasonable being endowed with the wondrous power of willing and choosing, He cannot force all this blessing on me, but waits until I give the willing consent of my heart. And the token of this consent He has, in His great kindness, ordered faith to be—that faith by which utter sinfulness casts itself into the arms of love to be saved, and utter weakness entrusts itself to be kept and made strong. What Infinite Love! The love with which the Father loved the Son! Love with which the Son loves us!

I can trust you; I do trust you. O keep me abiding in you, my loving Savior.

Abide As Christ Abides in the Father

As the Father loved Me, I also have loved you; continue in My love . . . you will abide in My love, just as I . . . abide in my Father's love.

John 15:9–10

Christ taught His disciples that to abide in Him was to abide in His love. The hour of His suffering is near, and He cannot speak much more to them. No doubt they have many questions to ask Him about His love and their abiding in Him. He anticipates and meets their wishes, and gives them His *own life* as the best expression of His command. As example and rule for abiding in His love, they only have to look to His abiding in the Father's love. In the light of His union with the Father, their union with Him will become clear. *His life in the Father is the law of their life in Him.*

The thought is so high that we can hardly take it in, and yet it is so clearly revealed that we dare not neglect it. Do we not read in John 6:57, "As I live because of the Father, *even so* he who feeds on Me will live because of me"? And the Savior prays so distinctly (John 17:22–23), "that they may be one *just as* We are one: I in them, and You in Me." The blessed union of Christ with the Father and His life in Him is the only rule of our thoughts and expectations in regard to living and abiding in Him.

Think first of *the origin* of that life of Christ in the Father. They were *one*—one in life and one in love. In this, His abiding in the Father had its root. Though dwelling here on earth, He knew that He was one with the Father, that the Father's life was in Him, and His love on Him. Without this knowledge, abiding in the Father and His love would have been utterly impossible for Christ. In the same way it is only in this knowledge that you can abide in Christ and His love. Know that you are one with Him—one in the unity of nature. By His birth He became man and took on your nature so that He might be one with you. By your new birth you become one with Him and are made partaker of His divine nature. The link that binds you to Him is as real and close as the one that bound Him to the Father—the link of a divine life. Your claim on Him is as sure as was His on the Father. Your union with Him is just as close.

And as it is the union of a divine life, it is one of an infinite love. In His life of humiliation on earth He tasted the blessing and strength of knowing himself to be the object of an infinite love, and He dwelt in it all through His days; from His own example He invites you to learn that in this the secret of your rest and joy can be found. You are one with Him: Yield yourself now to be loved by Him; let your eyes and heart open up to the love that shines and presses in on you on every side. Abide in His love.

Think also of *the form* of that abiding in the Father and His love that is to be the law of your life: "I have kept My Father's commandments and abide in His love" (John 15:10). His was a life of subjection and dependence and yet was most blessed. To our proud, self-seeking nature the thought of dependence and subjection suggests the idea of humiliation and servitude; but in the life of love lived by the Son of God, and to which He invites us, they are the secret to enjoying great blessing. The Son is not afraid of losing anything by giving up all to the Father, for He knows that the Father loves Him and can have no interest apart from that of the beloved Son. He knows that as complete as the dependence on His part so is the sharing on the part of the Father of all He possesses. Therefore, when He said, "The Son can do nothing of Himself, but what He sees the Father do"; He adds at once, "for whatever He (the Father) does, the Son also does in like manner. For the Father loves the Son, and shows Him all things that He Himself does" (John 5:19–20).

The believer who studies this life of Christ as the pattern and the promise of what his life may be learns to understand how "Without Me you can do nothing" (John 15:5) is the forerunner of "I can do all things through Christ who strengthens me" (Philippians 4:13). We learn to glory in weaknesses, to delight in hardships and difficulties for Christ's sake, for "when I am weak, then I am strong" (2 Corinthians 12:10). The apostle Paul rises above the ordinary tone in which so many Christians speak of their weakness. They are seemingly content to merely tolerate their state, while Paul sees much more; he has learned from Christ that in the life of divine love the emptying of self and the sacrifice of our will is the surest way to have all we could wish or want. Dependence, subjection, and self-sacrifice are for the Christian, as for Christ, the blessed path of life. Just as Christ lived through and in the Father, even so the believer lives through and in Christ.

Think of the *glory* of this life of Christ in the Father's love. Because He gave himself wholly to the Father's will and glory, the Father crowned Him with glory and honor. He acknowledged Him as His only representative; He made Him partaker of His power and authority; He exalted Him to share His throne as God. And even so will it be with him who abides in Christ's love. If Christ finds us willing to trust ourselves and our interests to His love, if in that trust we give up all care for our own will and honor, if we make it our glory to exercise and confess absolute dependence on Him in all things, if we are content to have no life but in Him, *He will do for us what the Father did for Him.* He will bestow His glory on us: As the name of our Lord Jesus Christ is glorified in us, we are glorified in Him (see 2 Thessalonians 1:12).

He acknowledges us as His true and worthy representatives; He entrusts us with His power; He admits us to His counsels as He allows our intercession to influence His rule of His church and the world; He makes us the vehicles of His authority and His influence over humankind. His Spirit knows no other dwelling than this, and seeks no other instruments for His divine work. What a blessed life of love awaits the soul that abides in Christ's love, even as He abides in the Father's!

Take and study Jesus' relationship to the Father as a pledge of what your own abiding can become. As blessed, as mighty, as glorious as was His life in the Father, so yours can be in Him! Let this truth, accepted under the teaching of the Spirit by faith, remove every element of fear that regards abiding in Christ a burden. In the light of His life in the Father, let it be from now on a blessed rest in union with Him, an overflowing fountain of joy and strength. To abide in His love—His mighty, saving, keeping, satisfying love, even as He did in the Father's love—can never be a work we have to perform; it must be with us as it was with Him, the result of the spontaneous outflow of a life from within.

All we need to do is to take time to study the divine image of this life of love set before us in Christ. We need to be quiet before God, gazing upon Christ's life in the Father until the light from heaven falls on it, and we hear the voice of our Beloved whispering gently to us the teaching He gave to the disciples. Soul, be still and listen; let every thought be hushed until the word has entered your heart: "Child, I love you, just as the Father loved Me. Abide in My love, even as I abide in the Father's love. Your life on earth in Me is to be the perfect counterpart of mine in the Father."

And if the thought comes: Surely this is too high for me; can it really be true? You must remember that the greatness of the privilege is justified by the greatness of the object He has in view. *Christ was the revelation of the Father on earth.* He could only be this because there was the most perfect unity, the most complete communication of all that the Father had to the Son. He could be His revelation because the Father loved Him, and He lived in that love. *Believers are the revelation of Christ on earth.* They can only be this when there is perfect unity; by this unity the world can know that He loves them. They are His representatives, His revelation to the world that Christ loves them with the infinite love that gives itself and all it has.

Lord, show us your love. Help us know with all the saints the love that passes knowledge. Lord, show us in your own blessed life what it is to abide in your love. And the sight will so win us that it will be impossible for us to seek, even for one single hour, any other life than the life of abiding in your magnificent love.

Obeying His Commandments

If you keep My commandments, you will abide in My love, just as I have kept My Father's commandments and abide in His love.

John 15:10

How clearly we are taught here the place that good works are to occupy in the life of the believer! Christ as the beloved Son was in the Father's love. He kept His commandments, and so *abode* in the Father's love. So the believer, without works, receives Christ and is in Him; he keeps the commandments and so *abides* in Christ's love. When the sinner, in coming to Christ, seeks to prepare himself by works, the voice of the Gospel sounds, "Not of works." Once in Christ, however, lest the flesh should abuse the word "Not of works," the Gospel lifts its voice as loudly to say, "Created in Christ Jesus *for good works*" (Ephesians 2:9–10). To the sinner out of Christ, works may be his greatest hindrance, keeping him from union with the Savior. To the believer in Christ, works are his strength and blessing, for by them faith is made perfect (James 2:22), the union with Christ is cemented, and the soul is established and more deeply rooted in the love of God. "If anyone loves Me, he will keep My word; and My Father will love him" (John 14:23). "If you keep My commandments, you will abide in My love."

The connection between keeping the commandments and abiding in Christ's love is easy to understand. Our union with Jesus Christ is not something of the intellect or sentiment, but a real, vital union in heart and life. The Holy Spirit breathes the holy life of Jesus, with His feelings and disposition, into us. The believer's calling is to think, feel, and will what Jesus thought, felt, and willed. Such a believer desires to be a partaker not only of the grace but also of the holiness of his Lord; or rather, he sees that holiness is the chief beauty of grace. To live the life of Christ means to him to be delivered from the life of self; the will of Christ is to him the only path of liberty from the slavery of his own self-will.

To the casual believer there is a great difference between the promises and the commands of Scripture. The former he counts his comfort and his food; but to the one who is really seeking to abide in Christ's love, the commands become no less precious. As much as the promises, they are the revelation of divine love, serving as guides into a deeper experience of the divine life; they are blessed helpers in the path to a closer union with the Lord. The harmony of our will with His will is one of the chief elements of our fellowship with Him. The will is the central faculty in the Divine as well as in human beings. The will of God is the power that rules the moral as well as the natural world.

How could there be fellowship with Him without delight in

His will? Of course, if salvation is to the sinner nothing but personal safety, then he can be careless or afraid of doing God's will. But as soon as Scripture and the Holy Spirit reveal to him the true meaning of salvation—the restoration to communion with God and conformity to Him—he realizes that there is no law more natural or more beautiful than this: Keeping Christ's commandments is the way to abide in Christ's love. His inmost soul approves when he hears his beloved Lord make the larger measure of the Spirit, with the manifestation of the Father and the Son in the believer, entirely dependent upon the keeping of His commandments (John 14:15–16, 21, 23).

There is another thing that opens to the sinner a deeper insight and secures a still more cordial acceptance of this truth. It is this: In no other way did Christ himself abide in the Father's love. In the life that Christ led on earth, obedience was a solemn reality. The dark and awful power that led humankind to revolt from God tempted Him too. To Him, as with all men, its offers of self-gratification were not matters of indifference; to refuse them, He had to fast and pray. He suffered, being tempted. He spoke very distinctly of *not* seeking to do His own will. This was a surrender He had to make continually. He made the keeping of the Father's commandments the distinct object of His life, and so did He abide in His love. He plainly tells us, "I do nothing of Myself; but as My Father has taught Me, I speak these things. And He who sent Me is with Me. The Father has not left Me alone, for I always do those things that please Him" (John 8:28–29). In this way He opened to us the only path to a blessed life on earth in the love of heaven; and when, as from our vine, His Spirit flows in the branches, keeping His commands is a sure sign of the life He inspires.

Believer, if you would abide in Jesus, be very careful to keep His commandments. Keep them in the love of your heart. Do not be content to have them in the Bible for reference, but have them transferred to the fleshy tables of your heart by careful study, by meditation and prayer, by a loving acceptance, and by the Spirit's teaching. Do not be content with the knowledge of some of the commands, those most commonly received among Christians, while others remain unknown and neglected. Surely, with your New Covenant privileges, you would not want to be behind the Old Testament saints who spoke so fervently: "Therefore *all* your precepts concerning *all* things I consider to be right" (Psalm 119:128). Be assured that there is still much of your Lord's will that you do not yet understand.

Make Paul's prayer for the Colossians yours, praying it for yourself and all believers: "that you may be filled with the knowledge of His will in all wisdom and spiritual understanding" (Colossians 1:9); and likewise, "labor fervently in prayers" as did wrestling Epaphras, "that you may stand perfect and complete in all the will of God" (Colossians 4:12). Remember that this is one of the great elements of spiritual growth—a deeper insight into the will of God concerning you. Do not imagine that entire consecration is the end; it is only the beginning of the truly holy life!

See how Paul, after having taught believers to lay themselves upon the altar as whole and holy burnt offerings to their God (Romans 12:1), immediately proceeds in verse 2 to tell them that true altar-life is becoming "transformed by the renewing of your mind, that you may prove what is that good and acceptable and perfect will of God." The progressive renewal of the Holy Spirit leads to growing like-mindedness to Christ; then comes a delicate power of spiritual perception—a holy instinct—by which the soul knows to recognize the meaning and the application of the Lord's commands to daily life in a way that remains hidden to the ordinary Christian. Keep the commandments of Christ dwelling richly within you; hide them within your heart, and you will taste the blessing of the man whose "delight is in the law of the Lord, and in His law he meditates day and night" (Psalm 1:2). Love will assimilate the commands into your inmost being as food from heaven. They will no longer come to you as a law standing outside and against you, but as the living power that has transformed your will into perfect harmony with all your Lord requires.

Keep them through strict obedience in your life, making it your solemn vow not to tolerate even a single sin. "I have sworn and confirmed that I will keep Your righteous judgments" (Psalm 119:106). Labor earnestly in prayer so that you may stand perfect and complete in all the will of God. Ask for the discovery of every secret sin—anything that is not in perfect harmony with the will of God. Walk faithfully and tenderly in the light you have, and yield yourself in an unreserved surrender to obey all that the Lord has spoken. When Israel took that vow, "All that the Lord has spoken we will do" (Exodus 19:8), all too soon they broke it. But the new covenant gives us the grace to make the vow and to keep it too (see Jeremiah 31). Be careful about disobedience even in little things. Disobedience dulls the conscience, darkens the soul, and deadens our spiritual energies. Therefore, keep the commandments of Christ with implicit obedience; be a soldier that asks for nothing but the orders of the commander.

And if even for a moment the commandments appear

grievous, just remember whose they are. They are the commandments of Him who loves you. They are all love; they come from His love and they lead to His love. Each new surrender to keep the commandments, each new sacrifice in keeping them, leads to deeper union with the will, the spirit, and the love of the Savior. The double reward promised in Scripture will be yours—a fuller entrance into the mystery of His love, a greater conformity to His own blessed life. And you will learn to prize these words as among your choicest treasures: "If you keep My commandments, you will abide in My love, just as I have kept My Father's commandments and abide in His love."

That Your Joy May Be Full

These things I have spoken to you that My joy may remain in you, and that your joy may be full.

John 15:11

Abiding fully in Christ is a life of exquisite and overflowing happiness. As Christ gets more complete possession of the soul, it enters into the joy of its Lord. His own joy, the joy of heaven, becomes its own in full measure, as an ever-abiding portion. Just as joy on earth is everywhere connected with the vine and its fruit, so joy is an essential characteristic of the life of the believer who fully abides in Christ, the Heavenly Vine.

We all know the value of joy. It alone is the proof that what we have really satisfies the heart. As long as duty, or self-interest, or other motives influence me, no one can know what the object of my pursuit or possession is really worth to me. But when it gives me joy, and they see me delight in it, they know that to me at least it is a treasure. So there is nothing quite so attractive as joy, no preaching so persuasive as the sight of hearts made glad. This makes gladness such a strong element in Christian character. There is no proof of the reality of God's love and the blessing He bestows, which people so quickly feel the strength of, as when the joy of God overcomes all the trials of life. And for the Christian's own welfare, joy is just as indispensable; the joy of the Lord is his strength (see Nehemiah 8:10), and confidence, courage, and patience find their inspiration in joy. With a heart full of joy no work can make us weary and no burden can depress us; God himself is our strength and song.

Let us hear what the Savior says about the joy of abiding in Him. He promises us *His own joy*: "My joy." As the whole parable refers to the life His disciples should have in Him after He ascended to heaven, the joy is that of His resurrection life. This is clear from other words of His in John 16:22: "I will see you again and your heart will rejoice, and your joy no one will take from you." It was only with the Resurrection and its glory that the power of the never-changing life began, and only in it that the never-ceasing joy could arise. With it was fulfilled the word: "Therefore God, even Your God, has anointed You with the oil of gladness more than Your companions" (Hebrews 1:9). The day of His crowning was the day of the gladness of His heart. That joy of His was the joy of a work fully and forever completed, the joy of the Father's presence regained, and the joy of souls redeemed. These are the elements of His joy, and abiding in Him makes us partakers of them.

The believer shares so fully Christ's victory and His perfect redemption that his faith can without ceasing sing the conqueror's song: "Thanks be to God who always leads us in triumph in Christ" (2 Corinthians 2:14). As the fruit of this, there is the joy of undisturbed dwelling in the light of the Father's love. And then, with this joy in the love of the Father, as a love received, we experience the joy of loving souls, as love going forth and rejoicing over the lost. Whether we look backward and see the work He has done, or upward and see the reward He has in the Father's love that passes knowledge, or forward in anticipation of continual joy experienced as sinners are brought home, His joy is ours. With our feet on Calvary, our eyes on the Father's face, and our hands helping sinners home, we have His joy as our own.

And then He speaks of this joy as *abiding*—a joy that is never to cease or be interrupted for a moment: "That My joy may remain in you." "Your joy no one will take from you." This is what many Christians cannot understand. Their view of the Christian life is that it is a succession of changes, sometimes joy and sometimes sorrow. And they appeal to the experiences of a man like the apostle Paul as proof of how much there may be of weeping, sorrow, and suffering. They have not noticed how Paul gives the strongest evidence to this unceasing joy. He understood the paradox of the Christian life as the combination at one and the same moment of all the bitterness of earth and all the joy of heaven.

He writes, "As sorrowful, yet *always rejoicing*" (2 Corinthians 6:10): These precious words teach us how the joy of Christ can overrule the sorrow of the world, can make us sing even while we weep, and can maintain in the heart, even when cast down by disappointment or difficulties, a deep consciousness of a joy that is unspeakable and full of glory (1 Peter 1:8). There is only one condition: "*I will see you again* and your heart will rejoice, and your joy no one will take from you." The presence of Jesus, distinctly manifested, cannot help but give joy. How can the soul not rejoice and be glad when it is abiding in Him consciously? Even when weeping for the sins and the souls of others, there is a fountain of gladness that springs up in us when we recognize His power and love to save.

And He wants His own joy abiding in us to be *full.* Jesus spoke three times of this full joy on His last night with the disciples. Once here in the parable of the Vine: "*These things I have spoken to you that your joy may be full*" (John 15:11); and every deeper insight into the wonderful blessing of being the branch of such a Vine confirms His Word. Then He connects it in John 16:24 with our prayers being answered: "*Ask and you will receive, that your joy may be full.*" To the spiritual mind, answered prayer is not only a means of obtaining certain blessings, but something infinitely higher. It is a token of our fellowship with the Father and the Son in heaven, of their delight in us, and our having been admitted and having a voice in that wonderful interchange of love in which the Father and the Son hold counsel and decide the daily guidance of the children on earth.

To a soul abiding in Christ, who longs for manifestations of His love and knows to take an answer to prayer in its true spiritual value—as a response from the throne to all its utterances of love and trust—the joy it brings is truly beyond words. The word of Jesus is found true: "Ask and you will receive, that your joy may be full." And then the Savior says, in His high-priestly prayer to the Father (John 17:13), "*These things I speak . . . that they may have My joy fulfilled in themselves.*" It is the sight of the great High Priest entering the Father's presence for us, ever living to pray and carry on His blessed work in the power of an endless life (see Hebrews 7:16) that removes every possible cause of fear or doubt and gives us the assurance and experience of a perfect salvation.

Let the believer who seeks, according to the teaching of John 15, to possess the full joy of abiding in Christ, and according to John 16, the full joy of prevailing prayer, press forward to John 17. Let him listen there to those amazing words of intercession spoken on his behalf, asking that his joy might be full. Let him, as he listens to those words, learn about the love that pleads even now for him in heaven without ceasing; let him take in the glorious objectives being pleaded for, and realize that by His all-prevailing pleading they are being accomplished. If the believer can do these things, Christ's joy will be fulfilled in him.

Christ's own joy, abiding joy, fullness of joy—this is the reward of the believer who abides in Christ. Why is it that this joy has so little power to attract? The reason, simply stated, is this: People, yes, even God's children, do not believe in it. Instead of looking upon abiding in Christ as the happiest life that ever can be led, it is regarded as a life of self-denial and of sadness. They forget that any self-denial and the sadness are the result of *not* abiding. To those who finally yield themselves unreservedly to abide in Christ for a bright and blessed life, their faith comes true—the joy of the Lord is theirs. The difficulties all arise from our refusal to surrender to full abiding.

Child of God, who seeks to abide in Christ, remember what the Lord says. At the close of the parable of the Vine He adds these precious words: "*These things* I have spoken to you that My joy may remain in you, and that your joy may be full." Claim the joy as part of the branch-life—not the first or main part, but the blessed proof of the sufficiency of Christ to satisfy every need of the soul. Be happy. Cultivate gladness. If there are times when it comes by itself, and the heart feels the unutterable joy of the Savior's presence, praise God for it and seek to maintain it. If at other times feelings are dull, and the experience of joy is not what you would wish, still praise God *for the life of unutterable blessing to which you have been redeemed.* In this, too, the word holds good: "According to your faith let it be to you" (Matthew 9:29). As you claim all the other gifts in Jesus, be sure to claim this one too—not for your own sake, but for His and the Father's glory. "*My joy* in you"; "that *My joy* may *remain* in you"; "*My joy fulfilled* in themselves"—these are Jesus' own words. It is impossible to take Him wholly and heartily, and not to get His joy too. Therefore, "Rejoice in the Lord always. Again I will say, rejoice!" (Philippians 4:4).

Showing Love to Fellow Believers

*This is My commandment, that you love one another
as I have loved you.*

John 15:12

"As the Father loved me, I also have loved you; continue in My love" (John 15:9). God became man; divine love began to run in the channel of a human heart; it became the love of man to man. The love that fills heaven and eternity is to be seen daily here in the life of earth and of time.

"This is My commandment," the Savior says, "That you love one another as I have loved you." He sometimes spoke of commandments, but love, which is the fulfilling of the law, is the all-including one and therefore is called His commandment—the new commandment. It is to be the great evidence of the reality of the new covenant, of the power of the new life revealed in Jesus Christ. It is to be the one convincing and indisputable token of discipleship: "*By this all will know* that you are My disciples" (John 13:35); "That they also may be one in Us, *that the world may believe*" (John 17:21); "That they may be made perfect in one, and *that the world may know* that You have sent Me, and have loved them as You have loved me" (v. 23). To the believer seeking perfect fellowship with Christ, the keeping of this commandment is both the blessed proof that he is abiding in Him and the path to a fuller, more perfect union with Him.

Let us try to understand how this is so. We know that God is love and that Christ came to reveal this, not as a doctrine but as a life. His life, in its wonderful self-abasement and self-sacrifice, was, above everything, the embodiment of divine love, which showed humankind in a way they could understand, how God loves. In His love to the unworthy and the ungrateful, in humbling himself to walk among men as a servant, in giving himself up to death, He lived and acted out the life of divine love that was in the heart of God. He lived and died to show us the love of the Father.

And now, just as Christ was to show forth God's love, believers are to show forth to the world the love of Christ. *They* are to prove to others that Christ loves them, and in loving fills them with a love that is not of earth. They, by *living and by loving just as He did*, are to be perpetual witnesses to the love that gave itself to die. Christ loved in such a way that even the Jews cried out at Bethany, "See how He loved him!" (John 11:36). Christians are to live so that men are compelled to say, "See how these Christians love one another." In their daily interactions with one another, Christians are "made a spectacle to the world, both to angels and to men" (1 Corinthians 4:9); and in the Christlikeness of their love to one another they are to prove what manner of spirit they are. In all the diversity of character, creed, language, or station in life, Christians are to prove that love has made them members of one body and of one another, and has taught them each to forget and to sacrifice self for the sake of the other. Their life of love is the primary evidence of Christianity, the proof to the world that God sent Christ and that He has shed abroad in them the same love with which He loved Him. Of all the evidences of Christianity, this is the most powerful and the most convincing.

This love of Christ's disciples to one another occupies a central position between their love for God and their love for their fellowmen. It is the test of their love to God, whom they cannot see. The love to one unseen may so easily be a mere sentiment, or even an imagination; but in the face-to-face dealings with God's children, love to God is really called into practice and shows itself in deeds that the Father accepts as done to himself. This is the only way that love for God can be proved to be true. Love to fellow believers is the flower and fruit of the root, unseen in the heart, of love to God. And this fruit again becomes the seed of love to all humankind; interaction with one another is the school in which believers are trained and strengthened to love their fellowmen who are as yet outside of Christ, not simply with cordiality that rests on points of agreement, but with the holy love that takes hold of the most unworthy, and bears with the most disagreeable for Jesus' sake. It is love to one another as disciples that is brought to the forefront as the link between love to God alone and to people in general.

In Christ's interaction with His disciples, this brotherly love finds the law of its conduct. As we study His forgiveness toward His friends—with the seventy times seven (Matthew 18:22) as its only measure—and look to His unwearied patience and His infinite humility, seeing the meekness and lowliness with which He seeks to win for himself a place as their servant who is wholly devoted to their interests, we can accept with gladness His command, "You should do as I have done" (John 13:15). Following His example, each lives not for himself but for the other. The law of kindness is on the tongue, for love has vowed that no unkind word will ever cross its lips. It not only refuses to speak but also not even to hear or think evil; the name and character of fellow Christians becomes even more important to protect than our own. My own good name I may leave to the Father; but my brother's or sister's my Father has entrusted to me. In gentleness and loving-kindness, in courtesy and generosity, in self-sacrifice and benevolence, in its life of blessing and of beauty, divine love, which has been shed abroad in the believer's heart (Romans 5:5), should shine out as it was displayed in the life of Jesus.

What is your response to such a glorious calling—to love like Christ? Does your heart leap at the thought of the unspeakable privilege of showing forth the likeness of eternal love? Or do you instead sigh at the thought of the inaccessible height of perfection to which you are called to climb? Christian, do not sigh at what is in fact the highest token of the Father's love, that He has called us to be like Christ in our love, just as He was like the Father in His love. Understand that the One who gave the command to abide in Him, gave the assurance that we only have to abide in Him to be able to love like Him. Accept the command as a new motive for fully abiding in Christ.

Regard abiding in Him more than ever as an abiding in His love. Rooted and grounded daily in a love that passes knowledge, you receive of its fullness and learn to love. With Christ abiding in you, the Holy Spirit pours out the love of God in your heart (Romans 5:5), and you love your fellow believers, even the most trying and unlovable, with a love that is not your own, but the love of Christ in you. And the command for you to love them is changed from a burden into a joy, if you can keep it linked, as Jesus linked it, to the command about His love for you: "Abide in my love; love one another as I have loved you" (John 15:10, 12).

"This is my commandment, that you love one another as I have loved you." This is some of the "much fruit" that Jesus promised we will bear—indeed, a cluster of the grapes of Eshcol, with which we can prove to others that the land of promise is indeed a good land (Deuteronomy 1:24–25). Let us try in all simplicity and honesty to translate the language of high faith and heavenly enthusiasm into the plain prose of daily conduct, so that all can understand it. Let our temperament be under the control of the love of Jesus: *He can* make us gentle and patient. Let the vow that not an unkind word about others shall ever be heard from our lips be laid trustingly at His feet. Let the gentleness that refuses to take offense, that is always ready to excuse, and to think and hope the best, mark our behavior with everyone.

Let the love that seeks not its own (1 Corinthians 13:5), but is always ready to wash others' feet (John 13), or even to give its life for them (John 15:13), be our aim as we abide in Jesus. Let our life be one of self-sacrifice, always studying the welfare of others, finding our highest joy in blessing others. And let us, in studying the divine art of doing good, yield ourselves as obedient learners to the guidance of the Holy Spirit. By His grace, the most commonplace life can be transformed with the brightness of heavenly beauty, as the infinite love of the divine nature shines out through our frail humanity.

"Abide in my love, and love as I have loved." Is this possible? Of course! We have the new holy nature, which grows ever stronger as it abides in Christ the Vine, and it can love as He did. Every discovery of evil in our old nature, every longing desire to obey the command of our Lord, every experience of the power and the blessing of loving with Jesus' love will urge us to accept with fresh faith our Lord's words: "Abide in Me, and I in you"; "Continue in My love."

That You Might Not Sin

In Him there is no sin. Whoever abides in Him does not sin.

1 John 3:5–6

"You know," the apostle John said in verse 5, "that He was manifested to take away our sins," and thereby indicated salvation from sin as the great object for which the Son was made man. The connection shows clearly that the "taking away" has reference not only to the Atonement and freedom from guilt but also to deliverance from the power of sin, so that the believer no longer practices it. It is Christ's personal holiness that constitutes His power to accomplish this purpose. He admits sinners into life-union with himself; the result is that their life becomes like His. "*In Him* there is no sin. Whoever abides *in Him* does not sin." As long as the believer abides, and as far as he abides, he does not sin. Our holiness of life has its roots in the personal holiness of Jesus. "If the root is holy, so (also) are the branches" (Romans 11:16).

The question at once arises: How is this consistent with what the Bible teaches about the continuing corruption of our human nature, or with what John tells us in 1 John 1:8, 10—

that if we say we have no sin, or have not sinned, we deceive ourselves and call God a liar? It is this passage that, if we look at it carefully, will teach us to understand our current text correctly. Note the difference in the two statements (v. 8), "If we say that *we have no sin*," and (v. 10), "If we say that *we have not sinned*." The two expressions cannot be equivalent; the second would then be merely a repetition of the first. *Having sin* in verse 8 is not the same as *practicing sin* in verse 10. *Having sin* means having a sinful nature.

The holiest believer must each moment confess that he has sin within him—namely, the flesh, in which dwells "no good thing" (Romans 7:18). Sinning or *practicing sin* is something very different: It is yielding to the indwelling sinful nature and falling into actual transgression. And so we have two admissions that every true believer must make. The one is that he still has sin within him (v. 8); the second is that sin has in former times broken out into sinful actions (v. 10).

No believer can make either statement: "I have no sin in me," or "I have in time past never sinned." If we say we have no sin at present, or that we have not sinned in the past, we deceive ourselves. But although we *have sin*, we need not confess that we are presently *practicing sin*; the confession of actual sinning refers to the past. It may, as appears from 1 John 2:2, be in the present also, but it is not *expected* to be. And so we see how the deepest confession of sin in the past (as Paul acknowledged his having been a persecutor of the church), and the deepest consciousness of still having a vile and corrupt nature in the present may coexist with humble but joyful praise to Him who keeps us from stumbling as we abide in Him.

But how is it possible that a believer, having sin in him—

sin of such intense vitality, and such terrible power as we know the flesh to have—can yet *not be practicing sin*? The answer is: "In Him there is no sin. He that abides in Him does not sin." When abiding in Christ becomes close and unbroken, so that the soul lives from moment to moment in perfect union with the Lord his keeper, He does, indeed, keep down the power of the old nature to such an extent that it does not regain dominion over him. We have seen that there are degrees in abiding. With most Christians the abiding is so weak and intermittent that sin continually obtains supremacy and brings the soul into subjection. The divine promise given to faith is: "Sin shall not have dominion over you" (Romans 6:14). But accompanying the promise is the command: "Do not let sin reign in your mortal body" (Romans 6:12).

The believer who claims the promise in full faith has the power to obey the command, and sin is kept from overpowering him. Ignorance of the promise, unbelief, or carelessness, however, opens the door for sin to reign. And so the life of many believers is a course of continual stumbling and sinning. But when a believer seeks full admission into a life of continual, permanent abiding in Jesus, the Sinless One, then the life of Christ can keep him from actual transgression. "In Him there is no sin. Whoever abides in Him does not sin." Jesus does save such a believer from his sin—not by the removal of his sinful nature, but by keeping him from yielding to it.

I have read of a young lion that could only be awed or kept down by the eye of his keeper. With the keeper anyone could come near the lion, and he would crouch—his savage nature still unchanged, thirsting for blood—trembling at the keeper's feet. You might even put your foot on his neck so long as the keeper was with you. But to approach him without the keeper would be instant death. In the same way, we can *have sin* and yet *not practice sin.* The evil nature, the flesh, is unchanged in its rebellion against God, but the abiding presence of Jesus keeps it under control. In faith the believer can entrust himself to the keeping, the indwelling, of the Son of God; as he abides in Him, he can count on Jesus to be there for him. It is union and fellowship with the Sinless One that is the secret of a holy life: "In Him there is no sin. Whoever abides in Him does not sin."

And now another question arises: Admitting that complete abiding in the Sinless One will keep us from sinning, is such abiding possible? May we hope to be able to so abide in Christ, even for one day, that we may be kept from actual transgressions? If the question is fairly stated and considered it will suggest its own answer. When Christ commanded us to abide in Him, and promised us such rich fruit-bearing to the glory of the Father, and such mighty power in our intercession, could He mean anything but the healthy, vigorous, complete union of the branch with the Vine? When He promised that as we abide in Him He would abide in us, could He mean anything else but that His dwelling in us would be a reality of divine power and love? Is not this way of saving from sin most glorifying to Him?

By keeping us on a daily basis humble and helpless in our consciousness of our evil nature, watchful and active in the knowledge of its terrible power, dependent and trustful in the remembrance that only His presence can keep the lion down— this gives all glory to Him and not to ourselves. O let us believe that when Jesus said, "Abide in Me, and I in you," He meant that, while we were not to be freed from the world and its tribulation, from the sinful nature and its temptations, we were at least to have this blessing fully secured to us—the grace to abide wholly, only, in our Lord. Abiding in Jesus makes it possible to keep from actual sinning; and Jesus himself makes it possible to abide in Him.

Dear Christian, I am not surprised if you find the promise of the text almost too high. Do not, however, let your attention be diverted by the question as to whether it would be possible to be kept for your whole life, or for so many years, without sinning. Faith only has to deal with the present moment. Ask this: Can Jesus at the present moment, as I abide in Him, keep me from those actual sinful acts that have been the stain and weariness of my daily life? You must say, "Surely He can." Take Him then at this present moment and say, "Jesus keeps me now; Jesus saves me now." Yield yourself to Him by earnest, believing prayer to be kept by His own abiding in you—and go into the next moment, and the succeeding hours, with this trust continually renewed. As often as the opportunity occurs in the moments between your activities, renew your faith in an act of devotion: Jesus keeps me now; Jesus saves me now. Let failure and sin, instead of discouraging you, only urge you to seek even more your safety by abiding in the Sinless One.

Abiding is a grace in which you can grow wonderfully, if you will but make a complete surrender, and then persevere with ever-increasing expectations. Regard it as *His* work to keep you abiding in Him and *His* work to keep you from sinning. It is indeed your work to abide in Him; but this is only possible because it is *His* work as the Vine to bear and hold you, the branch. Gaze upon *His holy human nature as something He prepared for you to be partaker of with himself,* and you will see that there is something even higher and better than being kept from sin—that is, the restraining from evil. There is the positive and larger blessing of now being a vessel purified and cleansed, filled with His fullness, and made a channel for showing forth His power, His blessing, and His glory.

He Is Your Strength

All authority has been given to Me in heaven and on earth.

Matthew 28:18

Be strong in the Lord and in the power of His might.

Ephesians 6:10

My strength is made perfect in weakness.

2 Corinthians 12:9

No truth is more generally admitted among sincere Christians than that they are utterly weak. Yet there is no truth more generally misunderstood and abused than this. Here, as elsewhere, God's thoughts are high above ours (Isaiah 55:8).

The Christian often tries to forget his weakness, but God wants us to remember it, and to feel it deeply. Christians want to conquer their weakness and to be freed from it; God wants us to rest and even rejoice in it. Christians mourn over their weakness, while Christ teaches His servants to say, "I take pleasure in infirmities; most gladly will I boast in my infirmities" (2 Corinthians 12:9–10). Christians think their weakness is the greatest hindrance in their life and service to God; but God tells us that rather than being a hindrance, our weakness is actually the secret of strength and success. It is our weakness, heartily accepted and continually realized, that gives us our claim and access to the strength of Him who has said, "*My strength* is made perfect *in weakness*."

When our Lord was about to take His seat upon the throne, one of His last statements was "All authority has been given to Me in heaven and on earth." Just as taking His place at the right hand of the power of God was something new and true—a real advance in the history of the God-man—so was His assuming all power and authority for heaven and earth. Omnipotence was now entrusted to the man Christ Jesus, so that from then on it might put forth its mighty energies through the channels of human nature. Here He connected this revelation of what He was to receive with the promise of the share that His disciples would have in it: When I am ascended, you will receive power from on high (Luke 24:49; Acts 1:8). It is in the power of the omnipotent Savior that the believer must find his strength for life and for work.

The disciples found this principle to be true. During ten days in the Upper Room they worshiped and waited at the footstool of His throne. They gave expression to their faith in Him as their Savior, their adoration of Him as their Lord, their love for Him as their Friend, and their devotion and readiness to work for Him as their Master. Jesus Christ was their one object of thought, of love, of delight. In such worship and devotion their souls grew up into intense communion with Him upon the throne, and when they were prepared, the baptism of power came. It was power within and power around them.

The power came to qualify them for the work to which they had yielded themselves—of testifying by life and word to their unseen Lord. With some the main testimony was to be that of a holy life, revealing heaven and the Christ from whom holiness came. The power came to set up the kingdom within them, to give them victory over sin and self, and to equip them by living experience to testify to the power of Jesus on the throne to make men live in the world as saints. Others were to give themselves up entirely to speaking in the name of Jesus. But all needed and all received the gift of power to prove that Jesus had received the kingdom of the Father. All power in heaven and earth was indeed given to Him, and by Him imparted to His people just as they needed it, whether for a holy life or effective service. They received the gift of power to prove to the world that the kingdom of God, to which they professed to belong, was "not in word but in power" (1 Corinthians 4:20). By having power within, they also had power around them, outside of themselves. For even those who would not yield themselves to the power of God felt its reality (Acts 2:43; 4:13; 5:13).

And what Jesus was to these first disciples, He is to us too. Our whole life and calling as disciples find their origin and their guarantee in the words: "All authority is given to Me in heaven and on earth." What He does in and through us, He does with almighty power. What He claims or demands, He works himself by that same power. All He gives, He gives with power and authority. Every blessing He bestows, every promise He fulfills, every grace He works—all is to be with power. Everything that comes from Jesus on the throne of power is to bear the stamp of power. The weakest believer may be confident that in asking to be kept from sin, to grow in holiness, to bring forth much fruit, he may count upon these his petitions being fulfilled with divine power. The power is in Jesus; Jesus is ours with all His fullness. It is in us, members of His body, that the power is to work and to be made known.

And if we want to know how the power is bestowed, the answer is simple: Christ gives His power in us by giving His life to us. He does not, as so many believers imagine, take the frail life He finds in them, and impart a little strength to help them in their frailty. No; it is in giving His own life to us that He gives us His power. The Holy Spirit came down to the disciples directly from the heart of their exalted Lord, bringing down into them the glorious life of heaven into which He had entered. And so His people are still taught to be strong in the Lord and in the power of His might (Ephesians 6:10). When He strengthens them, it is not by taking away the sense of weakness, and giving in its place the feeling of strength. Not at all.

Rather, in a very wonderful way He leaves and even increases the sense of utter impotence; along with it He gives them the consciousness of strength in Him. "We have this treasure in earthen vessels, that the excellence of the power may be of God and not of us" (2 Corinthians 4:7). The weakness and the strength are side by side; as the one grows, the other does, too, until his disciples understand the saying, "When I am weak, then am I strong; I boast in my infirmities, that the power of Christ may rest upon me" (2 Corinthians 12:9–10).

The believing disciple learns to look upon Christ on the throne, Christ the Omnipotent, as his life. He studies that life in its infinite perfection and purity, in its strength and glory; it is eternal life dwelling in a glorified man. And when he thinks of his own inner life, and longs for holiness, to live a life well-pleasing to God, or for power to do the Father's work, he looks up, and, rejoicing that Christ is his life, he confidently acts on the assurance that Christ's life will work mightily in him all he needs. In things both small and great, in being kept from sin from moment to moment, or in the struggle with some special difficulty or temptation, *the power of Christ* is the measure of his expectation. He lives a truly joyous and blessed life, not because he is no longer weak, but because, being utterly helpless, he consents and expects to have the mighty Savior work in him.

The lessons these thoughts teach us for practical life are simple but very precious. The first is that all our strength is in Christ, laid up and waiting for our use, according to the measure in which it finds the channels open. But whether its flow is strong or weak, whatever our experience of it may be, there it is in Christ: all authority in heaven and earth. Let us take time to study this. Let us get our minds filled with the thought: So that Jesus might be to us a perfect Savior, the Father gave Him all power and authority. That is the qualification that fits Him for our needs—having all the power of heaven that triumphs over all the powers of earth, including those in our heart and life.

The second lesson is: This power flows into us as we abide in close union with Him. When the union is weak, undervalued or undercultivated, the inflow of strength will be weak. On the other hand, when our union with Christ is praised as our highest good, and everything is sacrificed for the sake of maintaining it, His power will work in us: His strength "is made perfect in (our) weakness." Our one care must therefore be to abide in

Christ as our strength. Our one duty is to be strong in the Lord and in the power of His might.

Let our faith be expanded to appropriate the exceeding greatness of God's power in them that believe, *even that power* of the risen and exalted Christ by which He triumphed over every enemy (Ephesians 1:19–21). Let our faith consent to God's wonderful arrangement: nothing but weakness in us *as our own*, all the power in Christ, and yet within our reach as surely as if it were in us. Let our faith go beyond self and its life daily into the life of Christ, placing our whole being at His disposal for Him to work in us. Let our faith, above all, confidently rejoice in the assurance that He will, with His almighty power, perfect His work in us. As we abide in Christ, the Holy Spirit will work mightily in us, and we too will be able to sing, "The Lord is *my strength* and song" (Isaiah 12:2). "*I can do all things* through Christ who strengthens me" (Philippians 4:13).

It Is Not in Ourselves

In me (that is, in my flesh) nothing good dwells.

Romans 7:18

To have life in himself is the prerogative of God alone, and of the Son, to whom the Father has also given it. To seek life, not in itself, but in God, is the highest honor of the creature. To live in and to himself is the folly and guilt of sinful man; to live to God in Christ is the blessing of the believer. To deny, to hate, to forsake, and to lose his own life: such is the secret of the life of faith. "It is no longer I who live, but Christ lives in me" (Galatians 2:20); "Not I, but the grace of God which was with me" (1 Corinthians 15:10): This is the testimony of each one who has found out what it is to give up his own life and to receive instead the blessed life of Christ within. There is no path to true life, to abiding in Christ, other than the way taken by our Lord before us—through death.

At the beginning of the Christian life, very few see this truth. In the joy of pardon, they feel compelled to live for Christ and trust that with the help of God they will be able to do so. They are still ignorant of the terrible struggle of the flesh against

God and its absolute refusal in the believer to be subject to the law of God. They do not know that nothing but death, the absolute surrender to death of all that is of the old nature, will do if the life of God is to be manifested in them with power. But bitter experience of failure soon teaches them the insufficiency of what they know about Christ's power to save; deep heart-longings are awakened to know Him better. He lovingly points them to His Cross. He tells them that in the same way they exercised faith in His death as their substitute, and found their title to life, so there they will also enter into its fuller experience. He asks them if they are willing to drink of the cup He drank of—to be crucified and to die with Him. He teaches them that in Him they are indeed already crucified and dead, for at conversion they became partakers of His death. But what they need now is to give a full and intelligent consent to what they received before they understood it, by an act of their own choice to die with Christ.

This demand of Christ's is one of unspeakable solemnity. Many a believer shrinks back from it, having a hard time understanding it. For he has become so accustomed to a life of continual stumbling that he barely desires, and still less expects, deliverance. Holiness, perfect conformity to Jesus, unbroken fellowship with His love, can scarcely be counted distinct articles of his creed. Where there is not intense longing to be kept to the utmost from sinning, and to be brought into the closest possible union with the Savior, the thought of being crucified with Him can hardly be welcome. The only impression it makes is that of suffering and shame; such a Christian is content that Jesus bore the Cross and so won for him the crown he hopes to wear. But how differently the believer who is really seeking to abide fully in

Christ looks upon it. Bitter experience has taught him how, both in the matter of entire surrender and simple trust, his greatest enemy in the abiding life is *self*. First it refuses to give up its will; then again, by its working, it hinders God's work.

Unless this life of self, with its willing and working, can be displaced by the life of Christ, with *His* willing and working, abiding in Him will be impossible. And then comes the solemn question from Him who died on the cross: "Are you ready to give up self, even to the point of death?" You, a living person born of God, are already in Me; you are already dead to sin and alive to God, He explains. But are you ready now, in the power of this death, to give up self entirely to death on the cross, to be kept there until your self-will is conquered? The question is a heart-searching one. Am I prepared to say that my old self will no longer have a word to say; that it will not be allowed to have a single thought, however natural, not a single feeling, however gratifying, not a single wish or work, however right?

Is this really what He requires? Is not our nature God's handiwork, and may not our natural powers be sanctified to His service? They may and must indeed. But perhaps you have not yet seen how the only way they can be sanctified is that they be taken out from under the power of self and brought under the power of the life of Christ. Do not think that this is a work that you can do because you earnestly desire it and are one of His redeemed ones. No, there is no way to the altar of conse-cration but through death.

As you yielded yourself a sacrifice on God's altar as one alive from the dead (Romans 6:13; 7:1), so each power of your nature—each talent, gift, and possession that is really to be holiness to the Lord—must be separated from the power of sin and self, and laid on the altar to be consumed by the fire that is ever burning there. It is in the slaying of self that the wonderful powers with which God has fitted you to serve Him can be set free for a complete surrender to God and offered to Him to be accepted, sanctified, and used. And though, as long as you are in the flesh, there is no thought of being able to say that self is dead; yet when the life of Christ is allowed to take full possession, self can be so kept in its crucified place, and under its sentence of death, that it will have no dominion over you. Jesus Christ becomes your second self.

Believer, would you truly and fully abide in Christ? Then prepare yourself to part forever from self and not to allow it, even for a single moment, to have anything to say in your inner life. If you are willing to entirely give up self, and to allow Jesus Christ to become your life within you, inspiring all your thinking, feeling, and acting, in things temporal and spiritual, He is ready to take charge. In the fullest and widest sense the word *life* can have, He will be *your life*, extending His interest and influence to each one of the thousand things that make up your daily life. To do this He asks only one thing: Come away, out of self and its life; abide in Christ and He will be your life. The power of His holy presence will cast out the old life.

To this end give up self at once and forever. If you have never yet dared to do it, for fear you might fail, do it now, in view of the promise Christ gives you that His life will take the place of your old life. Try to realize that though self is not dead, you are indeed dead *to* self. Self is still strong and living, but it has *no power over you*. You, your renewed nature—you, your new self, born again in Jesus Christ from the dead—are indeed dead to sin and alive to God (Romans 6:11). Your death in

Christ has freed you completely from the control of self; it has no power over you, except as you, in carelessness or unbelief consent to yield to its usurped authority. Come and accept by faith the glorious position you have in Christ. Be of good courage, only believe; do not fear to take the irrevocable step, and to say that you have, once and for all, given up self to the death for which it has been crucified in Christ (Romans 6:6). And trust Jesus the Crucified One to hold self to the Cross and to fill its place in you with His own blessed resurrection life.

In this faith, abide in Christ! Cling to Him; rest on Him; hope in Him. Renew your consecration daily; daily accept afresh your position as one ransomed from your tyrant, and now in turn made a conqueror. Daily look with holy fear on the enemy, self, which struggles to free itself from the cross. Be aware that it seeks to allure you into giving it some little liberty, or else stands ready to deceive you by its profession of willingness now to do service for Christ. Remember, self that seeks to serve God is more dangerous than self that refuses to obey God. Look upon it with holy fear, and hide yourself in Christ; in Him alone is your safety. Abide in Him; He has promised to abide in you. He will teach you to be humble and watchful. He will teach you to be happy and trustful.

Bring every interest of your life, every power of your nature, all the unceasing flow of thought, will, and feeling that makes up life, and trust Him to take the place that self once filled so easily and so naturally. Jesus Christ will indeed take possession of you and dwell in you; and in the restfulness, peace, and grace of the new life, you will have unceasing joy at the wondrous exchange that has been made—the coming out of self to abide in Christ alone.

The Guarantee of the New Covenant

Jesus has become the guarantee of a better covenant.

Hebrews 7:22

Scripture speaks of the old covenant as not being faultless; God complains that Israel did not continue in it and so He disregarded them (Hebrews 8:7–9). The problem was that the old covenant did not secure its apparent object of uniting Israel and God: Israel had forsaken Him, and He had as a consequence disregarded Israel. Therefore, God promises to make a new covenant, free from the faults of the first, and able to accomplish its purpose. If it were to accomplish its end, it would need to secure God's faithfulness to His people, and His people's faithfulness to God. And the terms of the new covenant expressly declare that these two objects will be attained. "I will put My laws into their mind"; in this way God seeks to secure their unchanging faithfulness to Him. "Their sins and their lawless deeds I will remember no more" (see Hebrews 8:10–12); this will be the means of assuring His unchanging faithfulness to them. A pardoning God and an obedient people: These are the two parties who are to meet and be eternally united in the new covenant.

The most beautiful provision of this new covenant is that of the guarantee in whom its fulfillment on both parts is assured. Jesus was made the guarantee of the better covenant. To man He became the guarantee that God would faithfully fulfill His part, so that man could confidently depend upon God to pardon, accept, and never again forsake them. And to God He likewise became the guarantee that man would faithfully fulfill his part, so that God could bestow on him the blessing of the covenant. The way in which He fulfills His office is this: As one with God, and having the fullness of God dwelling in His human nature, Christ Jesus personally guarantees to men that God the Father will do what He has promised. As one with us, and having taken us up as members into His own body, He is a guarantee to the Father that His interests will be cared for. All that man must be and do is secured in Christ. It is the glory of the new covenant that it has in the Person of the God-man its living guarantee, its everlasting security. And it can be easily understood how, in proportion as we abide in Him as the guarantee of the covenant, its objects and its blessings will be realized in us.

We will understand this best if we consider it in the light of one of the promises of the new covenant: "I will make an everlasting covenant with them, that *I will not turn away from doing them good*; but I will put My fear in their hearts so that *they will not depart from Me*" (Jeremiah 32:40).

With what wonderful condescension the infinite God here bows to our weakness! He is the Faithful and Unchanging One, whose word is truth; and yet to show more abundantly to the heirs of the promise how unchanging is His counsel, He binds himself in the covenant to remain faithful: "I will make an everlasting covenant, that I will not turn away from doing them good." Blessed is the man who has thoroughly appropriated this and finds his rest in the everlasting covenant of the Faithful One!

But in a covenant there are two parties. And what if man becomes unfaithful and breaks the covenant? Provision must be made, if the covenant is to be well ordered in all things and sure, that this cannot happen. Man can never undertake to give such an assurance but God provides for this too. He not only undertakes in the covenant that He will never turn from His people but also pledges to put His fear in their hearts so that they will not depart from Him. In addition to His own obligations as one party in the covenant, He undertakes for the other party too: "I will put My Spirit within you and cause you to walk in My statutes, and *you will keep* My judgments and do them" (Ezekiel 36:27). Blessed is the man who understands this part of the covenant as well! He sees that his security is not in the covenant that he makes with his God, for he would likely break it continually. He finds that a covenant has been made in which God stands good, not only for himself, but also for all humankind. He grasps the blessed truth that his part in the covenant is to accept what God has promised to do, and to expect the sure fulfillment of God's plan to secure the faithfulness of His people: "I will put My fear in their hearts so that *they will not depart from Me.*"

It is here that the blessed work of the Guarantor comes in to secure the covenant, appointed of the Father to see to its maintenance and perfect fulfillment. To Christ Jesus the Father has said, "I will give You as a covenant to the people" (Isaiah 42:6). And the Holy Spirit testifies, "All the promises of God in Him are Yes, and in Him Amen, to the glory of God through us" (2 Corinthians 1:20). The believer who abides in Him has divine assurance for the fulfillment of every promise of the covenant.

Christ was made the guarantee of a better covenant. It is as our Melchizedek that Christ is this guarantee (see Hebrews 7). Aaron and his sons passed away; of Christ it is witnessed that *He ever lives*. He is a priest in the power of an *endless life*. Because He *continues forever*, He has an unchangeable priesthood. And because He *ever lives* to make intercession, He can "save to the uttermost" all who come to Him (Hebrews 7:25). It is because Christ is the Ever-Living One that His guarantee of the covenant is so effectual. He ever lives to make intercession and can therefore save completely. Every moment the unceasing pleadings rise up from His holy presence to the Father, the unceasing pleadings that secure for His people the powers and the blessings of the heavenly life. And every moment from Him flows out the mighty influences of His unceasing intercession toward His people, continually conveying to them the power of the heavenly life. As guarantee with us for the Father's favor, He never ceases to pray and present us before Him; as guarantee with the Father for us, He never ceases to work and reveal the Father within us.

The mystery of the Melchizedek priesthood, which the Hebrews were not able to receive (Hebrews 5:10–14), is the mystery of resurrection life. It is in the Resurrection that the glory of Christ as guarantee for the covenant consists: He ever lives. He performs His work in heaven in the power of a divine, omnipotent life. He ever lives to pray; there is not a moment that as our guarantee His prayers do not ascend to secure the Father's fulfillment of the covenant to us. He performs His work on earth in the power of that same life; there is not a moment that His answered prayers—the powers of the heavenly world—do not flow downward to secure for His Father our fulfillment of the New Covenant. In the life that is eternal there are no breaks, never a moment's interruption; each moment has the power of eternity in it. He every moment lives to pray. Every moment He lives to bless. He can, therefore, save to the uttermost, completely and perfectly.

Believer, come and see here how the possibility of abiding in Jesus every moment is secured by the very nature of this ever-living priesthood of your guarantee. Moment by moment, as His intercession rises up, its effectiveness descends. And because Jesus stands good for fulfilling the covenant—"I will put My fear in their hearts so that they will not depart from me"—He cannot afford to leave you a single moment to yourself. He dare not do so, or He fails in His undertaking. Your unbelief may fail to realize the blessing, but He cannot be unfaithful. If you will consider Him, and the power of that endless life after which He was made and serves as High Priest, your faith will arise to believe that an endless, ever-continuing, unchangeable life of abiding in Jesus awaits you.

It is as we see what Jesus is, and is to us, that abiding in Him will become the natural and spontaneous result of our knowledge of Him. If His life unceasingly, moment by moment, rises to the Father for us and descends to us from the Father, then to abide moment by moment is easy, even simple. Each moment of conscious communion with Him let us say, "Jesus, our guarantor, keeper, ever-living Savior, in whose life I live, I abide in you." Each moment of need, darkness, or fear, we still say, "Great High Priest, in the power of an endless, unchangeable life, I abide in you." And for the moments when direct and distinct communion with Him must give way to necessary earthly activities, we can trust Him to be our guarantee. His unceasing priesthood, with its divine effectiveness and the power with which He saves to the uttermost, will keep us abiding in Him still.

The Glorified One

Your life is hidden with Christ in God. When Christ who is our life appears, then you also will appear with Him in glory.

Colossians 3:3–4

The one who abides in Christ, the Crucified One, learns what it is to be crucified with Him, and in Him to be dead to sin. The one who abides in Christ, the Risen and Glorified One, becomes a partaker of His resurrection life and the glory He is now crowned with in heaven. Unspeakable are the blessings that flow out of our union with Jesus in His glorified life.

This life is a life of *perfect victory and rest.* Before His death, the Son of God had to suffer and struggle, could be tempted and troubled by sin and its assaults. But as the Risen One, He has triumphed over sin; and, as the Glorified One, His humanity has participated in the glory of Deity. The believer who abides in Him as such is led to see how the power of sin and the flesh are indeed destroyed; the consciousness of complete and everlasting deliverance becomes increasingly clear, and blessed rest and peace—the fruit of such a conviction that victory and deliverance are an accomplished fact—take possession of the life. Abiding in Jesus, in whom he has been raised and set in heavenly places (Ephesians 2:6), such a believer receives that glorious life streaming from the Head through every member of the body.

This life is a life in *the full fellowship of the Father's love and holiness.* Jesus often gave prominence to this thought with His disciples. His death was a return to the Father. He prayed: "O Father, glorify Me together *with Yourself,* with the glory which I had *with You* before the world was" (John 17:5). As the believer, abiding in Christ the Glorified One, seeks to realize and experience what His union with Jesus on the throne implies, he understands how the unclouded light of the Father's presence is His highest glory and blessing, and in Christ it is the believer's portion too. He learns the sacred art of always, in fellowship with His exalted Head, dwelling in the secret place of the Father's presence. When Jesus was on earth, temptation could still reach Him, but in glory that is done away with. Everything is holy there and in perfect harmony with the will of God. And so the believer who abides in Him experiences the awesome fact that in this high fellowship his spirit is sanctified into growing harmony with the Father's will. The heavenly life of Jesus is the power that casts out sin for him.

This life is a life of *loving goodness and activity.* Seated on His throne, Christ dispenses His gifts, bestows His Spirit, and never ceases to lovingly watch and work for those who are His. The believer cannot abide in Jesus the Glorified One without feeling himself stirred and strengthened to work; the Spirit and the love of Jesus breathe into him the will and the power to be a blessing to others. Jesus went to heaven with the objective of obtaining power there to bless abundantly. As the Heavenly

Vine, He does this work only through the medium of His people as His branches. Therefore, whoever abides in Him, the Glorified One, bears much fruit, because he receives of the Spirit the power of his exalted Lord's eternal life. The humblest believer can become the channel through which the fullness of Jesus, who has been exalted to be a Prince and a Savior, flows out to bless those around him.

There is one more thought in regard to this life of the Glorified One, and ours in Him. It is a life of *wondrous expectation and hope.* Christ sits at the right hand of God, *waiting in expectation* till all His enemies are made His footstool (Hebrews 10:13), looking forward to the time when He will receive His full reward, when His glory will be known to all, and His beloved people will be with Him forever in that glory. The hope of Christ is also the hope of His redeemed: "I will come again and receive you to Myself; that where I am, there you may be also" (John 14:3). This promise is as precious to Christ as it ever can be to us. The joy of meeting is surely no less for the coming Bridegroom than for the waiting bride. The life of Christ in glory is one of longing expectation; the full glory only comes when His beloved people are with Him.

The believer who abides closely in Christ will share with Him in this spirit of expectation. Not so much for the increase of personal happiness, but from the spirit of enthusiastic allegiance to his King, he longs to see Him come in His glory, reigning over every enemy, the full revelation of God's everlasting love. "Till He comes" is the watchword of every truehearted believer. "When Christ who is our life appears, then you also will appear with Him in glory" (Colossians 3:4).

There may be serious differences in the understanding of

His promised coming. To one it is plain as day that He is coming very soon in person to reign on earth, and that imminent coming is his hope and his stay. To another, who loves his Bible and his Savior just as much, the coming can mean nothing but the Judgment Day—the solemn transition from time to eternity, the close of history on earth, the beginning of heaven; and the thought of that manifestation of his Savior's glory is his joy and his strength. It is Jesus, Jesus coming again, Jesus taking us to himself, Jesus adored as Lord of all, that is important; He is the sum and the center of the whole church's hope.

It is by abiding in Christ the Glorified One that the believer can fully anticipate, in true spiritual longing, His coming, which alone brings true blessing to the soul. There is an interest in the study of the end times, and such schools sadly are often better known by their contentions about opinions and condemnation of believers who do not agree with them than by the meekness of Christ's character. It is only the humility that is willing to learn from those who may have other gifts and deeper revelations of the truth than we, the love that always speaks gently and tenderly of those who do not see as we do, and the heavenly character that shows that the Coming One is indeed already our life, that will persuade either the church or the world that our faith is not in the wisdom of men but in the power of God.

To testify of the Savior as the Coming One, we must be abiding in and bearing His image as the Glorified One. Not the correctness of the views we hold, nor the earnestness with which we advocate them, will prepare us for meeting Him, but only our abiding in Him. Only then can our manifestation in glory with Him be what it is meant to be: a transfiguration, a breaking out and shining forth of the indwelling glory that only awaited the day of revelation.

Blessed is the life "hidden with Christ in God, set in the heavenly places in Christ," abiding in Christ the glorified! Once again the question comes: Can a frail child of dust really dwell in fellowship with the King of Glory? And again the blessed answer has to be given: To maintain that union is the very work for which Christ has all power and authority in heaven and on earth at His disposal. The blessing will be given to him who will trust his Lord for it, the one who in faith and confident expectation continually yields himself to be wholly one with Him. It was an act of wondrous though simple faith by which the soul first yielded itself to the Savior. That faith grows up to gain clearer insight and a surer hold on God's truth that we are one with Him in His glory. In that same wondrously simple but wondrously mighty faith, the soul learns to abandon itself entirely to the keeping of Christ's almighty power and the merits of His eternal life. Because it knows that it has the Spirit of God dwelling within to communicate all that Christ is, it no longer looks upon it as a burden or even an effort, but allows God's divine life to have its way, to do its work; its faith is the increasing abandonment of self, the expectation and acceptance of all that the love and the power of the Glorified One can perform. In that faith, unbroken fellowship is maintained and growing conformity to His image realized. As with Moses, the fellowship makes us partakers of the glory, and our lives begin to shine with a brightness not of this world.

What a blessed life! *It is* ours, for Jesus is ours. We have the possession within us in its hidden power, and we have the prospect before us in the manifestation of its full glory. May our daily lives be the bright and blessed proof that a hidden power dwells within, preparing us for the glory to be revealed. May our abiding in Christ the Glorified One be our strength to live to the glory of the Father, our enabling to share in the glory of the Son.

And now,
little children,
abide in Him,
that when He appears, we may have
confidence and not be ashamed
before Him at His coming.
1 John 2:28